ON THE TRAIL OF THE
DINOSAURS

ON THE TRAIL OF THE DINOSAURS

DR MICHAEL BENTON

Kingfisher Books

A QUARTO BOOK

This edition first published in 1989
by Kingfisher Books, Grisewood & Dempsey Limited
Elsley House, 24-30 Great Titchfield Street, London W1P 7AD.

British Library Cataloguing in Publication Data
Benton, Michael, 1956-
   On the trail of the dinosaurs.
   1. Dinosaurs
   I. Title
   567.9'1

ISBN 0-86272-498-8

This book was designed and produced by
Quarto Publishing plc
6 Blundell Street
London N7 9BH

Senior Editor: Kate Kirby
Editor: Steve Parker

Designer: Peter Laws

Illustrators: Graham Rosewarne, Jim Robins, Janos Marffy,
Sally Launder, Kevin Maddison and David Kemp

Picture research: Irene Lynch

Art Director: Nick Buzzard
Assistant Art Director: Chloë Alexander
Editorial Director: Carolyn King

Typeset in Great Britain by QV Typesetting Ltd, London
Manufactured in Hong Kong by Regent Publishing Services Limited
Printed in Hong Kong by South Sea Int'l Press Ltd.

Special thanks to Karin Skonberg

CONTENTS

An early summary of the history of life and the history of the earth, published as a print about 1880 (right). The successive layers of sedimentary rocks are shown on the right, with igneous intrusions at the base. On the left is shown the well-known succession of life forms from simple seaweeds and jellyfish at the bottom, through trees, amphibians, flying and swimming reptiles, to mammoths and other early mammals.

CAINOZOIC OR TERTIARY.

MESOZOIC OR SECONDARY.

PALÆZOIC OR PRIMARY.

EOZOIC OR ARCHÆAN.

IGNEOUS ROCKS.

Pleistocene
Glacial Drifts
Pliocene
Miocene
Oligocene
Eocene

Chalk

Gault
Neocomian
Oolite

Clays and limestone

Lias (mostly Blue Clay)

Penarth shales
Keuper marls
Bunter Sand- stone
Permian (dolomite and Sand)

Coal Measures (Shales and sandstones with seams of coal)

Millstone Grit

Carboniferous Limestone

Devonian (Limestones & Shales &c)

Old Red Sandstone

Silurian (limestones & shales)

(Ordovician some lime- stone shales tuffs & slates &c)

Cambrian Slates flag stones & grits &c

Pebidian
Arvonian
Dimetian

Plutonic Rocks

Intrusive Rocks
Porphyries
Basalts
Granites
Greenstones &c

CAINOZOIC OR TERTIARY.

MESOZOIC OR SECONDARY.

PALÆZOIC OR PRIMARY.

EOZOIC OR ARCHÆAN.

IGNEOUS ROCKS.

1. SIVATHERIUM	5. PTERODACTYLUS	9. CARBONIFEROUS FERN	13. ACANTHODUS	17. ZOSTERITES
2. MASTODON LONGIROSTRIS	6. AMMONITES	10. LEPIDODENDRON	14. DIPLACANTHUS	18. AMMONITES
3. ELEPHAS PRIMIGENIUS	7. PLESIOSAURUS	11. CALAMITES	15. LEPIDOSTEUS	19. GONIATITES
4. PALÆOTHERIUM	8. ICHTHYOSAURUS	12. LABYRINTHODON	16. CLIMATIUS	20. STROPHOMENA

INTRODUCTION

For more than a century, dinosaurs have held an equal fascination for scientists and for members of the public, young and old alike. The giant fossilized bones of dinosaurs and other extinct animals discovered in the rocks of Europe and North America, in particular, have played central roles in many key scientific controversies, especially during the early years when geology and zoology became distinct as sciences. Is the Earth really ancient? Have animals become extinct? Did evolution take place? Today, dinosaurs are no less important in their scientific role at the centre of palaeobiology, the study of how ancient organisms lived and evolved. There is still a great deal to learn.

The first recorded dinosaur find was made in the 17th century. Robert Plot, the Keeper of the Ashmolean Museum in Oxford, England, was sent an unusual and very large fossil bone from a quarry in the parish of Cornwell, Oxfordshire. He published an illustration of it in his *Natural History of Oxford-shire, being an Essay toward the Natural History of England* in 1676, and speculated about what it might be. He argued that it was a real bone, or the remains of one, and not a mere "sport of nature" created by some unknown forces within the Earth's crust. In Plot's day, many naturalists explained the fossilized shells and bones buried in the rocks as instruments of the Devil, set there to delude us about the veracity of the Bible, or as chance rock formations that just happened to look like modern shells or bones. Plot would have none of this, and saw that the outline shape, and the internal porous structure, were so like modern bone that any other explanation would be nonsensical.

The first dinosaur fossil to be illustrated: the knee end of a thigh bone of Megalosaurus, *found in Oxfordshire and described by Robert Plot in 1676 (above). It was later named* Scrotum humanum, *an unlikely interpretation!*

Further, Plot surmised correctly that the specimen was the lower end of a thigh bone (the knee end) of some giant animal. He wrote: "It must have belong'd to some greater animal than either an Ox or Horse; and if so (say almost all other authors in the like case) in probability it must have been the bone of some Elephant brought hither during the government of the Romans in Britain."

Plot was not happy with this argument, however. One reason was the lack of documentary evidence that the Romans ever brought elephants to Britain. A second reason was that he had seen a living elephant on show in Oxford in 1676, and had observed that its bones would be much larger than the specimen from Cornwell parish. He went on to give historical information on the skeletons of giant human remains found in church burial grounds, and referred to the many biblical, historical and mythological records of giants. The present specimen must, then, "have been the bones of Men or Women . . . notwithstanding their extravagant magnitude."

Plot's illustration allows us to identify his specimen as the lower end of the thigh bone of *Megalosaurus*, a meat-eating dinosaur that has since been found fairly frequently in Oxfordshire rocks of the Middle Jurassic period. However, some years after its discovery, his find was given a most peculiar interpretation and name. In 1763, R Brookes, in his *The Natural History of Waters, Earths, Stones, Fossils and Minerals with their Virtues, Properties and Medicinal Uses*, named it *Scrotum humanum* in view of its shape, and despite its excessive size. Strictly, this is the first scientific name ever given to a dinosaur species. We should refer to *Megalosaurus* as *Scrotum*, and to the Megalosauridae (an important family of early meat-eating dinosaurs) as the Scrotidae! Fortunately, Brookes' name was not used by other palaeontologists at the time, and it soon sank into decent obscurity.

Science and religion

During the 18th century, more dinosaur remains were collected in Europe, but they raised little interest. Naturalists had shifted their attention to the more spectacular remains of giant animals from the Pleistocene period — the mammoths, mastodons, giant ground sloths and others from the great Ice Ages of the past million years or so. These remains were easy to excavate in many cases, lying as they did in loose, soft rocks or openly in caves, and they were often remarkably complete. A great debate raged in the latter half of the 18th century: Were these the remains of extinct animals, or did such large creatures still survive today in unexplored parts of the world, like Australia, central Asia or South America? The argument was tied up with many complex scientific and theological issues, and it was central to several great issues of the day.

The key question was how to reconcile the Bible and science. Was the Bible to be understood literally, or should it be taken as an allegory of the history of the Earth? In 1650, Archbishop James Ussher, Archbishop of Armagh and Primate of Ireland, calculated the exact date of the creation of the Earth as 23 October, 4004 BC. His calculations were based on the ages of the patriarchs and other textual evidence from the Bible. John Lightfoot, a distinguished Greek scholar who was Vice Chancellor of Cambridge University, had arrived at a slightly later date, 3928 BC, in his 1644 calculation; he even gave the time as nine o'clock on the morning of 17 September. Ussher's date came to be accepted, and it was printed in the marginal notes of English bibles after 1701. Were the naturalists of the 18th century to accept this date?

Scientific evidence that the Earth was much older than 6,000 years was mounting all the time, yet most naturalists were loath to overthrow the biblical basis of society by speaking out strongly against a strict literary interpretation of its events. The evidence included problems in imagining how all the species of living plants and animals could have fitted into the Ark (at the time, new species were being found at an increasing rate), in understanding how the complexities of the Earth's surface geology could have been formed in such a short time, and in explaining the increasing numbers of extinct plants and animals coming to light.

The geological evidence seemed overwhelming. Geologists such as James Hutton, a Scottish farmer and amateur naturalist, observed the cycles of nature whereby great mountains slowly rose up and were then worn away. He saw how the high Scottish hills were being eroded by rain, frost and wind on top; how the rock fragments were washed into small streams, and on into larger rivers; and finally into the sea, where they were deposited as sand sediments and eventually formed the sedimentary rock sandstone. He saw huge thicknesses of sandstone in the rocks and argued that these must have been formed over vast spans of time by the same processes we see at work today. This was his Principle of Uniformitarianism, whereby uniform kinds and scales of processes acted in the past as they do today. But such a notion demanded great lengths of time in the history of the Earth.

Extinction and creation

The question of extinction was resisted by many scientists even into the early 19th century, but eventually most of them gave way to the mounting evidence. The world was becoming more fully explored: Captain Cook found no living mammoths or mastodons in Australia, and other explorers detected no trace of such creatures in the depths of Asia or Africa. In addition, the diversity of prehistoric animals was increasing yearly. There were strange fossil crocodiles from the coast of Yorkshire in northern England, buried deep within the rock; there were exquisitely preserved lizard-like and bat-like creatures from the slate quarries of central Germany; and there were trackways of giant footprints from Europe and North America.

The issue was settled to the satisfaction of most scientists by the brilliant work of Baron Georges Cuvier of the Paris Museum, from the 1790s to the 1830s. Cuvier showed how to reconstruct the original

fossil types that could be used to recognize particular geological formations, wherever they occurred; the associations gave way to others as they ascended the pile of sediments. The scientific applications of these principles soon became clear, and the science of stratigraphy was born.

Enter the dinosaurs

In the 1820s, the first dinosaurs were properly described from their fossils. There was none of the talk of elephants and giant humans that beset the writings of Plot and other earlier naturalists. The fossil bones could be dated as being, for example, from the Jurassic or Cretaceous periods of geological time, on the basis of associated fossil shells, plants and fishes. They were identified immediately as being the remains of extinct animals. Some bones of a large meat-eating reptile were excavated from the "slate" mines of Stonesfield in Oxfordshire and sent to the Reverend Professor William Buckland around 1820. He accumulated sufficient remains to determine that the animal was a meat-eater and a reptile. Buckland named it *Megalosaurus*, meaning "giant lizard", in 1824 — the first scientifically named dinosaur (barring *Scrotum*, of course!). One year later a Sussex family doctor and keen geologist, Gideon Mantell, named *Iguanodon*, on the basis of a few teeth found by his wife, and limb bones excavated from Cretaceous sandstones and mudstones in a quarry at Cuckfield, Sussex. Both Buckland and Mantell interpreted their finds as the remains of giant lizards, and they made tentative reconstructions of the whole animals along those lines: slender sprawling limbs, long narrow body, and a very long tail. Not surprisingly, their size estimates were spectacular: Mantell estimated at one stage that *Iguanodon* might have been 30 metres or more in length. (Present measurements from complete skeletons are closer to 10 metres, although there are some 30-metre dinosaurs as well.)

appearance of the skeleton of an extinct animal by applying the rules of comparative anatomy — the system of matching similar parts of the body between diverse living species. He produced dramatic life-like restorations of the great fossil mammals then known, and argued powerfully that the history of life had been punctuated many times by local extinctions. Whole assemblages of plants and animals flourished for a while, and then were wiped out because of a change of climate or some other stress.

Certain geologists took up Cuvier's idea that extinction was a normal event in our world's past, and developed a theory in which major catastrophes controlled most aspects of the history of the Earth and its life. Their main contribution was to emphasize another key fact of geology, the Law of the Superposition of Strata. This rather grand title says something quite simple: if left undisturbed, the oldest strata (layers) of sedimentary rocks are at the bottom of the pile, the youngest at the top.

Geological surveyors were finding regular patterns in the distribution of fossils. Where they found the bones of extinct reptiles, they also found ammonites (extinct, coiled relatives of snails). Where they found particular types of oysters, they also found specific kinds of corals. There were regular associations of

Fossil collecting in England in the 1820s: the chalk pit at Cherry Hinton, Cambridgeshire (top), and the quarry at Cuckfield, Sussex (above), where the first partial skeleton of Iguanodon *was excavated.*

Several more dinosaurs were named in the 1830s, from England and Germany. Most naturalists continued to regard them as exotic giant lizards, and no more. Richard Owen, a brilliant young anatomist and palaeontologist, was given the task of surveying all that was known about fossil reptiles. He presented his

An early reconstruction of Iguanodon *based on a model on show at the Natural History Museum in London, dating from 1895 (above left).*

A cartoon of Sir Richard Owen (1804-92), an eminent student of dinosaurs in Victorian England (above).

report to the British Association for the Advancement of Science in 1841, in a paper that lasted for about three hours. He concluded, in reference to *Megalosaurus, Iguanodon* and the other "giant lizards", the following: "The combination of such characters, some, as the sacral ones, altogether peculiar among reptiles, others borrowed, as it were, from groups now distinct from each other, and all manifested by creatures far surpassing in size the largest of existing reptiles, will, it is presumed, be deemed sufficient ground for establishing a distinct tribe or suborder of Saurian Reptiles, for which I would propose the name of Dinosauria."

With these words, the dinosaurs ("terrible lizards") were born. It took a brilliant leap of this kind to allow palaeontologists to recognize the dinosaurs for what they were: not giant lizards, or bizarre oversized monsters, but a distinctive and formerly highly successful group of animals, the like of which does not exist today. Owen went on in his paper to argue that the dinosaurs were massive animals, more akin in their adaptations to elephants and rhinoceroses than to the modern lizards. He did not mean that they were related to these mammals in an evolutionary way, but that they had similar adaptations of physiology and locomotion to those seen in modern large animals.

Owen was trying to make an additional point which has now been largely forgotten. One of his key motives in arguing a seemingly "modern" view of the dinosaurs — that they had many features of advanced mammalian biology — was to suggest that modern reptiles are degenerate remnants of a once great group. He was at odds with the strongly held belief of his day, progressionism, in which the pattern of life has run from simple to complex kinds of organisms through time. In arguing for the degeneration of the reptiles through time, he hoped to counter the evidence that life had "progressed" in some way.

The views of progressionism did not necessarily entail evolution, of course — although they did for many. The progressive pattern of the fossil record could be explained by a succession of Divine creations, each terminated by a flood or some other catastrophe. However, evolution was much talked about at the time, following the advanced writings of enlightened 18th-century French naturalists such as Buffon and Lamarck. But no satisfactory mechanism for evolution had yet been proposed.

In the context of evolution

In 1859, Charles Darwin published his *On the Origin of Species*. In this monumental work he made a powerful case for natural selection as the mechanism of evolution: the best-adapted organisms of each generation are selected to survive and breed, and their offspring inherit their advantageous features. Darwin had next to nothing to say about dinosaurs, but he did cite the progresssive pattern of the fossil record as evidence for this theory. Only two years later, however, dinosaurs entered the evolution story.

In 1860, a fossil feather was found in the Upper Jurassic rocks of quarries near Solnhofen, southern Bavaria. One year later, a nearly complete bird skeleton came to light in the same area. The news spread throughout the international scientific community, which was alerted to the immense value of the specimen since it was by a long way the oldest known fossil bird, and it also had unusual anatomical features. These showed a mixture of primitive reptile characteristics and advanced bird features. For example, it

PROFESSOR MARSH'S PRIMEVAL TROUPE.
HE SHOWS HIS PERFECT MASTERY OVER THE CERATOPSIDÆ.
(*See Proceedings of the British Association at Leeds.*)

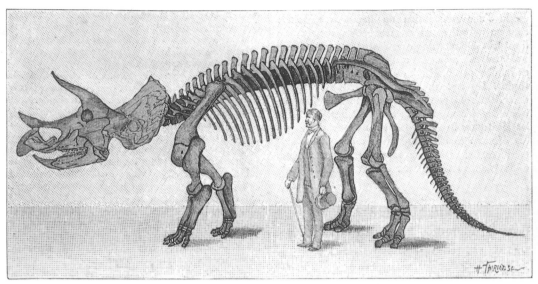

had teeth in the jaws, claws on the hands, and a long bony tail, just like a reptile; but it also had wings, feathers, large eyes, and a wishbone (furcula), just like a modern bird. The skeleton was assigned to the genus *Archaeopteryx*, established in 1861.

Amid much international bargaining, Owen secured the specimen for the British Museum for £700, twice his annual acquisitions budget. It soon became clear that *Archaeopteryx* was an evolutionary intermediate stage or "missing link" between reptiles and birds. Thomas Huxley, another eminent English anatomist and palaeontologist, used it as strong evidence in favour of the Darwinian notion of evolution. He explicitly proposed that *Archaeopteryx* was a feathered dinosaur, a view seemingly close to most modern interpretations. If the feathers had not been preserved with the bones of *Archaeopteryx*, it would probably have been identified as a small meat-eating dinosaur.

Dinosaurs were central to many of the fundamental scientific debates of the past two centuries, yet little was known about them at the time. In the latter half of

Othniel Marsh (1831-99), a leading North American dinosaur expert (above). He was famed for his research on the remarkable extinct mammals of the midwest of the United States (top left), as well as for his collecting and restoration of such well-known dinosaurs as Triceratops *(top right).*

the 19th century, great collections of dinosaur bones were made in the "badlands" of the American midwest by the great bonehunters, Edward Cope and Othniel Marsh. Many of the well-known dinosaurs, seen in museums and paintings, were named by them: *Allosaurus, Stegosaurus, Triceratops,* and *Tyrannosaurus.* This century, large collections of newly-discovered dinosaurs have been made in the old hunting grounds of Europe and North America, as well as on nearly every other continent. In addition, and probably more importantly, palaeontologists have become involved in a broad range of studies of the life and times of the dinosaurs, in attempts to achieve a detailed understanding of how these "other-worldly monsters" lived and why they were so successful. This book tells the story of how dinosaurs are collected and studied, and gives detailed insights into some of the key research problems that are being investigated by dinosaurian palaeobiologists into the 1990s.

Michael Benton

Michael Benton
Belfast, 3 May 1989.

CHAPTER ONE

WHAT ARE THE DINOSAURS?

Dinosaurs are an extinct group of reptiles, known only from fossils. The words "dinosaur" and "fossil" have pejorative meanings in common speech — a "dinosaur" is someone or some organization that has outlived its usefulness; a "fossil" is a dried-up, boring old person. So why do so many people find dinosaurs fascinating?

Dinosaurs answer the child in all of us; they stretch the imagination and excite our wonder. How could they have been so big? How long did they live? Why did they die out? It is a sad and dry person, indeed a "fossil", who does not stand back in wonder at the thought of a 27-metre-long *Diplodocus* or a huge *Tyrannosaurus* with teeth like steak knives.

Dinosaurs seem to interest people of all ages and nationalities. Every few weeks, it seems there are more headlines in the newspapers about the discovery of a new dinosaur skeleton in some remote part of the world, or the proposition of a new theory about how the dinosaurs behaved or why they died out. Indeed, dinosaurs have proved to be a useful vehicle for news reports on almost anything to do with evolution or the history of life. The word "dinosaur" in a headline is enough to attract readers. This is as true in countries where spectacular dinosaur skeletons are found fairly frequently, such as the United States, Canada, and the Soviet Union, as in places, such as Britain, where new dinosaurs are only rarely found.

Dinosaur skeletons are often the most exciting exhibits in museums. This skeleton of the plant-eater Iguanodon *(above) attracted the wonder of late Victorian museum-goers in London, in 1895.*

Outside Washington's Smithsonian Institute, children queue up to play on a life-like model of Triceratops *(right).*

Palaeontologists, the scientists who study the fossils of dinosaurs and other extinct animals and plants, are motivated by many of the child-like questions mentioned above. The pleasures of studying dinosaurs are manifold: the excitement of prospecting for bones, the drama of discovery, the painstaking excavation of the bones, their preparation and cleaning in the laboratory, the analysis of how the animal lived, and the mixture of science and art that goes into the reconstruction of what the creature looked like in life. These are the themes of the present book.

What is a dinosaur?

It is generally true that dinosaurs are big reptiles. The name "dinosaur" means "terrible reptile", and that is a fair summary of the impression they make on us. The largest dinosaurs were the biggest land animals of all time. They included the long-necked herbivorous sauropods such as *Diplodocus* and *Barosaurus*, which reached lengths of 27 metres — as long as three buses parked nose to tail — and *Brachiosaurus*, which stood 12 metres tall when it stretched its head upwards in giraffe fashion. In size, these giants rivalled the largest whales in our present-day oceans. This is remarkable since water acts to support the vast bulk of a whale, yet the dinosaurs lacked that support. The largest living land animals today, the elephants, weigh up to five tonnes; but this is almost negligible compared to the estimated weight of *Brachiosaurus*, at 78 tonnes.

The carnivorous dinosaurs also achieved enormous size. *Tyrannosaurus* was 15 metres long, six metres high, and had

ruthlessly efficient meat-cutting teeth 18 centimetres long. It was the largest terrestrial meat-eater of all time.

Dinosaurs were not all monsters, however. Many of the carnivores were agile, lightweight hunters, no larger than a human child, which fed on lizards and mouse-sized mammals. The smallest, *Compsognathus*, was up to 90 centimetres long and may have weighed as little as three kilograms — some specimens were no larger than a chicken.

On balance dinosaurs were bigger than mammals. The average size for all dinosaurs considered together would have been just larger than a human, while the average for all mammals would be about one-tenth of this. The big mammals such as elephants, rhinos and hippos are more than outweighed by the fact that most mammals are small shrews, bats, mice and other rodents.

The dinosaurs form a natural group, or clade, that had a single common ancestor. They were a single, and at times flourishing, side branch of the great evolutionary tree that includes all living and extinct plants and animals. This fact has only been appreciated in the last few years, as a result of rigorous new analyses of the features (characters) of the

bones and teeth from dinosaurs and their extinct relatives.

Nearly every dinosaur book offers vague statements about the origin of the dinosaurs: for example that they arose from several different ancestors, and these ancestors are not clearly known, and so the dinosaurs are merely an assemblage of large fossil reptiles, convenient for popular perception, but not really a single, natural group and interesting as such to the professional palaeontologist. Views have changed radically because of the application of a new technique of analysing evolutionary trees, called cladistic analysis, and also because of new finds and examinations of the special features of the archosaurs, the larger group of reptiles, of which the dinosaurs form a major part.

Cladistic analysis

Biologists and palaeontologists assume that life evolved through a succession of stages, represented in the fossil record, towards the present-day diversity of 10-30 million species of plants and animals. A great deal of evidence shows that all present-day organisms are related to each other, and that all of them — forms as diverse as slime

New dinosaurs are being found all the time. This spectacular sauropod, Mamenchisaurus, *(left) is the result of recent excavations in China, which have turned up dozens of new species quite different from the better-known dinosaurs of Europe and North America.* Mamenchisaurus *has the longest neck of any known animal — at 11 metres.*

Putting dinosaur sizes into perspective. Most dinosaurs were on a scale several times larger than typical modern animals. A well-known big dinosaur, Diplodocus *(1), towers over a human being (2) drawn to the same scale. There were some human-sized dinosaurs, however, as well as a few turkey-sized forms such as* Compsognathus *(3).*

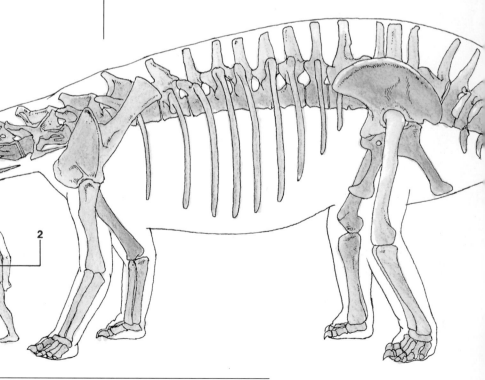

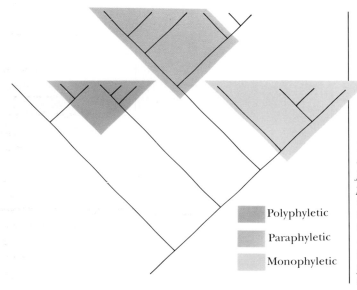

moulds and elephants, oak trees and beetles — ultimately arose from a single common ancestor, some 3,500 million years ago (see page 29). This means a single evolutionary tree, or phylogeny, relates all organisms, living and extinct, to each other.

Thousands of scientists around the world are currently engaged in the task of establishing exactly what that phylogeny looks like. The task is huge. If there are up to 30 million species alive today, how many species must have existed over the past 3,500 million years? If the average duration of a species is between one and 10 million years, the total must be massive. Hence, individual scientists or groups devote themselves to establishing the shape of small parts, the "twigs", of the tree.

The two main techniques of phylogenetic analysis in use today had their origins in the 1960s, but only now are they coming into full effect. One technique is molecular phy-

The principles of cladistic analysis, a relatively new tool for determining evolutionary patterns of living and extinct organisms. The aim is to find monophyletic groups, or clades, that include all descendants of a single common ancestor (left), rather than paraphyletic or polyphyletic groups, which are said to be "unnatural" groups.

Polyphyletic

Paraphyletic

Monophyletic

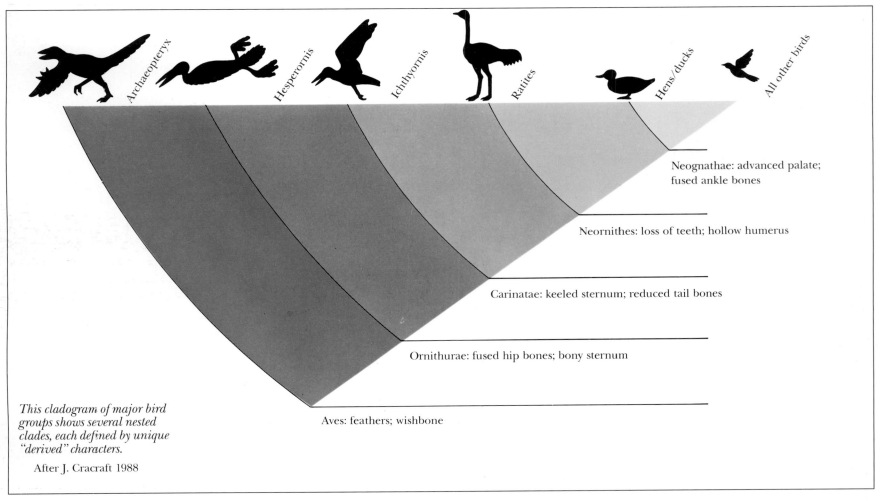

Neognathae: advanced palate; fused ankle bones

Neornithes: loss of teeth; hollow humerus

Carinatae: keeled sternum; reduced tail bones

Ornithurae: fused hip bones; bony sternum

Aves: feathers; wishbone

This cladogram of major bird groups shows several nested clades, each defined by unique "derived" characters.

After J. Cracraft 1988

logeny reconstruction: the comparison of similar molecules from different species in order to determine how closely related they are, or more specifically, how long ago they shared their most recent common ancestor. This technique cannot be applied to long-extinct forms such as the dinosaurs, since their flesh has long since rotted away and even the molecular structure of their bones has broken down. The second technique of phylogeny reconstruction, cladistic analysis must be used instead.

Cladistic analysis is the search for monophyletic groups, or "clades". A clade is a group that includes all the descendants of a single ancestor. Such groups are marked by the possession of at least one unique feature — a character that the common ancestor acquired and passed on to all of its descendants. Feathers are a familiar example of the character that defines the bird group. Feathers are complex outgrowths from the skin made from keratin, a flexible protein; they may have evolved from reptilian scales, which are also made from keratin. The possession of feathers can be said to define a bird: it is "synapomorphy", a unique character derived from the common ancestor and shared by the descendants (a unique, shared, derived character). The first bird, *Archaeopteryx*, had feathers, as shown by its remarkably well-preserved fossils.

The key to cladistic analysis is to consider characters carefully, since many characters are not synapomorphies, and hence do not define clades.

In carrying out a character analysis, the first step for the cladist is to distinguish between derived characters and primitive characters. For example, all birds have a pair of eyes. Is this a synapomorphy of birds? Clearly not, since many animals besides birds have two eyes. This can be established by comparisons with an "outgroup", which in this

(Cont page 20.)

ARCHAEOPTERYX

Archaeopteryx *("ancient wing") is arguably the most famous fossil of all. The first specimen was a feather, in 1860. Since then, six skeletons have been collected, the last one reported only in 1988. All specimens were found in the vicinity of Solnhofen, southern Bavaria, in the so-called lithographic limestones. The fine-grained quality of these limestones has preserved numerous fossils beautifully, often with soft parts intact. They include jellyfish, worms, plants, fish skins and guts, the delicate hollow bones of* Archaeopteryx *and even its feathers.* Archaeopteryx *shows several synapomorphies (unique derived features) of the class Aves (Birds), such as feathers, wings and fused clavicles (the "wishbone").*

DINOSAUR FAMILY TREE

The evolutionary tree of dinosaurs contains a great deal of information. The horizontal axis represents time, and the vertical axis represents dinosaurian diversity. All the major families of dinosaurs are indicated with horizontal lines that record their known distribution in time, as based upon present fossil evidence. Future finds of dinosaur skeletons may extend the time ranges backwards or forwards in time.

There are two "fixed" time lines that do not seem to be breached, however. The dinosaurs arose from a single ancestor some 230 million years ago, in the Middle to Late Triassic, and it is unlikely that older dinosaur skeletons will be found. The second "fixed" time line corresponds to the extinction of the last dinosaurs 66 million years ago. Despite strenuous efforts to find post-Mesozoic dinosaur specimens, and many reports of supposed discoveries, no such remains have withstood close scrutiny. Most usually, post-mesozoic dinosaur bones have been reworked, that is, removed from the rock by natural erosion and redeposited in a younger sediment.

The most important aspect of this phylogenetic tree is the representation of the relationships between the different families. This is based on recent cladistic analyses, carried out by a number of North American and European vertebrate palaeontologists after 1985, and the pattern shown here is largely accepted. However, the tree here is quite revolutionary in the sense that it is dramatically different from anything that was available before 1985, and from anything in popular books of this sort. It is also important because it shows a much higher degree of *resolution* than the earlier phylogenies; that is, the pattern of relationships is shown in a much more detailed way than was possible before.

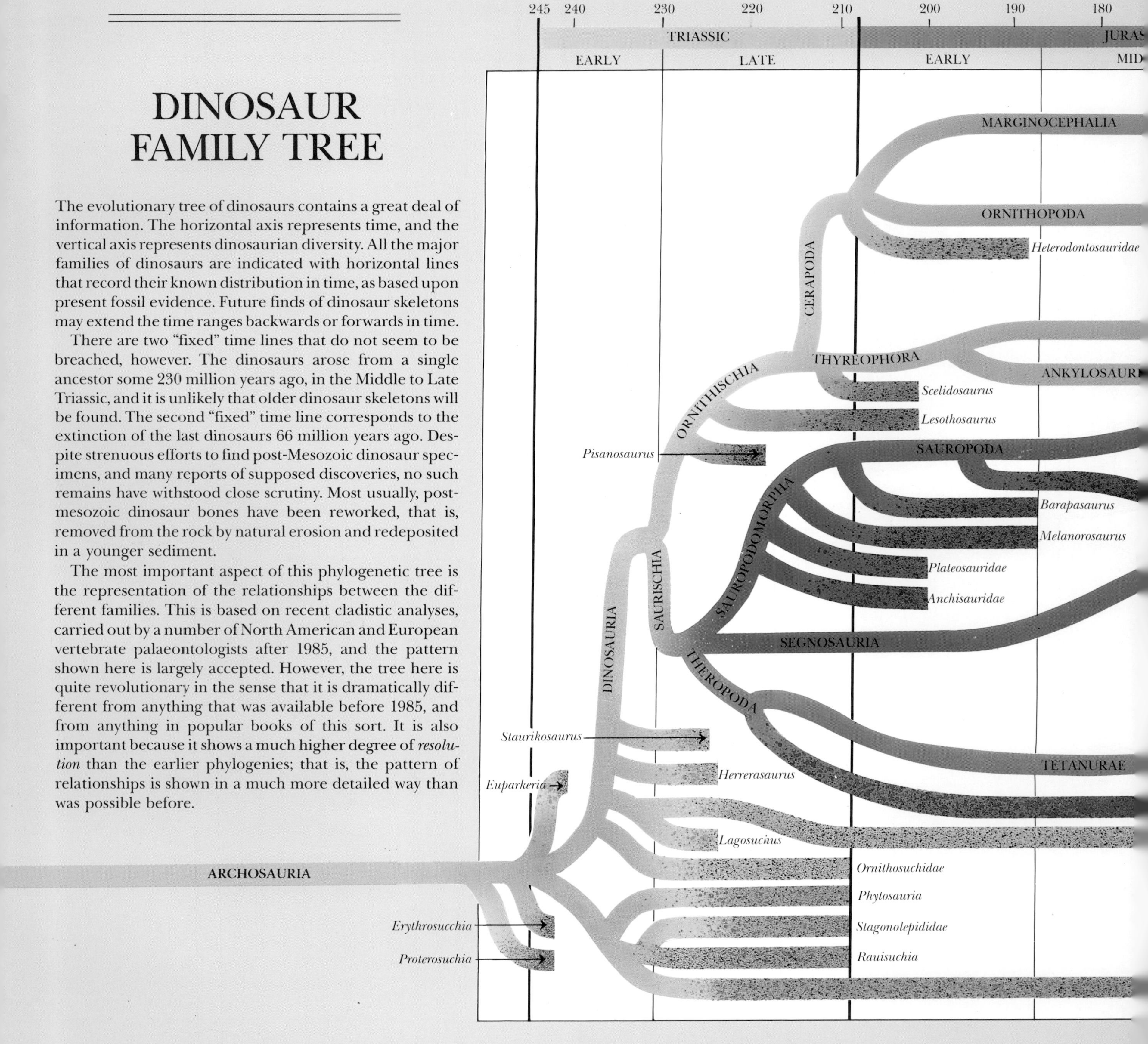

245 240 230 220 210 200 190 180

TRIASSIC JURAS

EARLY LATE EARLY MID

MARGINOCEPHALIA

ORNITHOPODA

Heterodontosauridae

CERAPODA

THYREOPHORA

ANKYLOSAURI

ORNITHISCHIA

Scelidosaurus

Lesothosaurus

Pisanosaurus

SAUROPODA

SAUROPODOMORPHA

Barapasaurus

Melanorosaurus

Plateosauridae

SAURISCHIA

Anchisauridae

SEGNOSAURIA

DINOSAURIA

THEROPODA

Staurikosaurus

TETANURAE

Euparkeria

Herrerasaurus

Lagosuchus

ARCHOSAURIA

Ornithosuchidae

Phytosauria

Erythrosucchia

Stagonolepididae

Proterosuchia

Rauisuchia

18

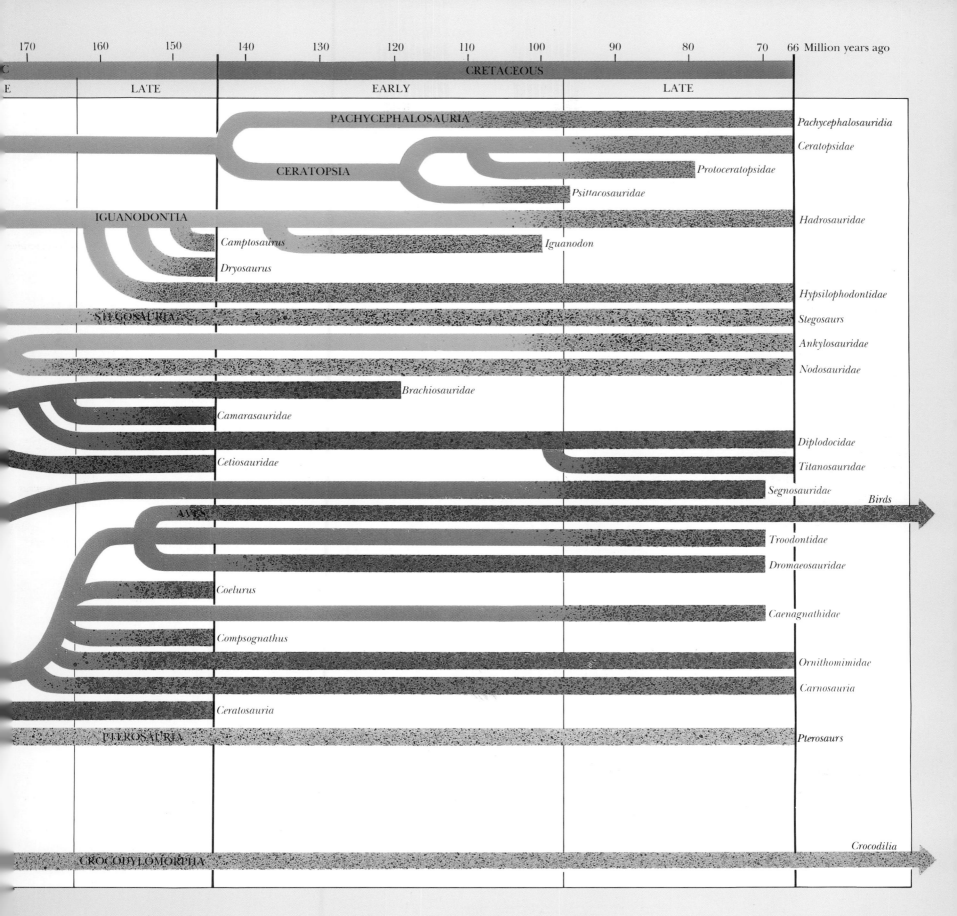

170   160   150   140   130   120   110   100   90   80   70   66 Million years ago

CRETACEOUS

E   LATE   EARLY   LATE

PACHYCEPHALOSAURIA   Pachycephalosauridia

Ceratopsidae

CERATOPSIA   Protoceratopsidae

Psittacosauridae

IGUANODONTIA   Hadrosauridae

Camptosaurus   Iguanodon

Dryosaurus

Hypsilophodontidae

STEGOSAURIA   Stegosaurs

Ankylosauridae

Nodosauridae

Brachiosauridae

Camarasauridae

Diplodocidae

Cetiosauridae   Titanosauridae

Segnosauridae

Birds

AVES

Troodontidae

Dromaeosauridae

Coelurus

Caenagnathidae

Compsognathus

Ornithomimidae

Carnosauria

Ceratosauria

PTEROSAURIA   Pterosaurs

Crocodilia

CROCODYLOMORPHA

case would consist of fish, frogs, and mammals. Characters are all submitted to outgroup comparison. "Possession of feathers" passes the outgroup comparison test as a synapomorphy of birds, since no fish, frog or mammal has feathers. "Possession of two eyes" fails the test as a synapomorphy of birds since all members of the outgroup share this character as well.

When carrying out a cladistic analysis, the boundaries for any particular study are drawn in a broad way, and then an intensive search for characters is made among all of the species within the group under scrutiny. The characters are tested by outgroup comparisons to find the synapomorphies, and the species are then arranged in a tree-like branching diagram called a cladogram. The cladogram represents relationships or recency of common ancestry *only*, so that all species, living and extinct, are placed in a row. A cladogram has no time scale.

The first well-known archosaur, Proterosuchus, *from the Early Triassic of South Africa and other continents (below). This animal probably looked like a moderate-sized crocodile, with its long jaws lined with sharp teeth, low skull, long tail and short legs.* Proterosuchus *shows the archosaurian synapomorphies of flat-sided teeth (rather than round in cross-section), an antorbital fenestra (the hole between nostril and eye socket), and a fourth trochanter (flange or ridge) on the femur (thigh bone).*

Common ancestors are then postulated at each dichotomous (two-way) branching point, and each of these branching points, or nodes, is defined by one or more synapomorphies. A node can be thought of as the evolutionary acquisition of a specific character, such as feathers. Everything "above" a node is a descendant of the hypothetical common ancestor. In effect, there is a succession of triangular-shaped clades. This "nesting" feature of clades is typical of cladograms.

The cladogram is converted into a phylogenetic tree by the addition of a time scale and the correct placing of the groups in chronological sequence. Usually the order of the fossils as they appear in the rocks matches the order of appearance of groups in the cladogram, but this is not always the case. Gaps in the fossil record mean we do not always know the oldest representatives of a particular group, and it would be wrong to assume that they did not

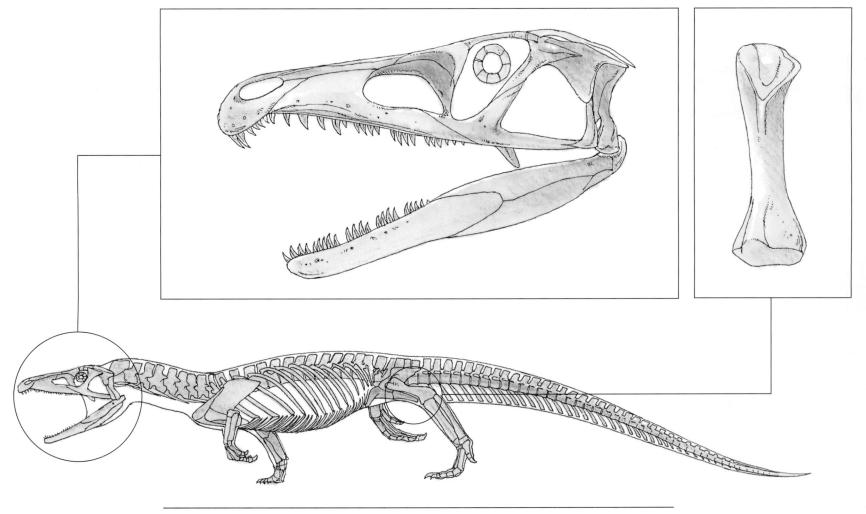

exist because we have not yet found them. This is why synapomorphies have to be tested by outgroup comparison rather than simply by following the order of appearance of characters in the fossil record.

The archosaurs

Archosaurs, or "ruling reptiles", include living crocodiles and birds, as well as the extinct dinosaurs, pterosaurs (flying contemporaries of the dinosaurs) and the "thecodontians", a ragbag group that includes the ancestors of all the other archosaurs.

The archosaurs arose some 250 million years ago, as far as we can tell. The first group, the proterosuchids, spread nearly worldwide. Their fossils are known from the Soviet Union, southern Africa, Antarctica, Australia, India, China and South America. They show the archosaur synapomorphies, seen in all archosaurs, but in no other animals: an

antorbital fenestra (a particular hole in the skull), recurved flat-sided teeth and a fourth trochanter on the femur (a specific ridge on the thigh bone).

During the Triassic period, some 245-208 million years ago, the archosaurs radiated (evolved and diversified) as moderately successful carnivores and gave rise to one herbivorous group. The Triassic "thecodontians" split into two main lineages. One included the superficially crocodile-like phytosaurs, the herbivorous aetosaurs (which also looked rather like crocodiles, but had snub noses for rooting up plant food, and narrow leaf-like teeth) and the often massive, carnivorous rauisuchians. Finally, in the Late Triassic, this lineage sprouted some lightweight bipedal (two-legged) animals that probably fed on insects and small lizard-like animals. These were, perhaps surprisingly, the first crocodilians. The group adopted its amphibious, quadrupedal (four-legged) fish-eating exist-

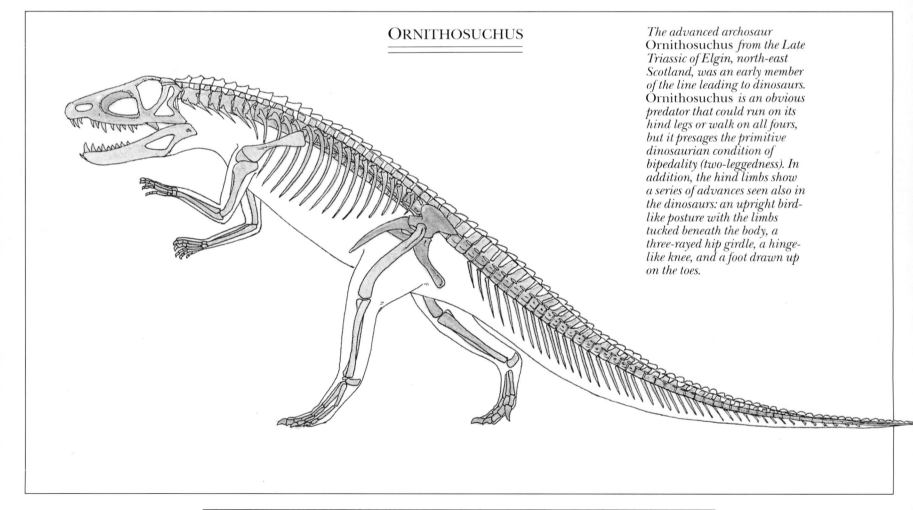

ORNITHOSUCHUS

The advanced archosaur Ornithosuchus *from the Late Triassic of Elgin, north-east Scotland, was an early member of the line leading to dinosaurs.* Ornithosuchus *is an obvious predator that could run on its hind legs or walk on all fours, but it presages the primitive dinosaurian condition of bipedality (two-leggedness). In addition, the hind limbs show a series of advances seen also in the dinosaurs: an upright bird-like posture with the limbs tucked beneath the body, a three-rayed hip girdle, a hinge-like knee, and a foot drawn up on the toes.*

ence only some 20 million years later, after the extinction of the phytosaurs.

The second archosaur lineage included active carnivores such as *Ornithosuchus*, which could walk quadrupedally or bipedally, and the lightweight *Lagosuchus*, which was a biped. These animals are so close to being dinosaurs in many features, it now seems remarkable that many scientists had denied it until recently. *Lagosuchus*, in particular, shows a long list of "dinosaur" characters: its bipedal posture; the long limbs with the shin bones (tibia and fibula) longer than the femur; the perforated acetabulum (the bowl-like depression in the hip bone that receives the ball-shaped end of the femur); the inturned head of the femur (the beginnings of the full right-angled femur head seen in dinosaurs and in a different form in mammals); the straight knee joint; the reduced hinge-like ankle joint (technically termed the advanced mesotarsal, or AM, ankle); the long

The carnivorous Riojasuchus *(above) had a powerful skull with deep jaws, showing adaptations to feeding on other land-based prey rather than fish.* Riojasuchus *and its relatives have often been confused with dinosaurs, but they fall on the crocodilian line of evolution.*

Lagosuchus *(right), from the Middle Triassic of Brazil, is so close to being a dinosaur that it fails to make the grade by only a few seemingly minor features. This small animal probably fed on insects and lizard-sized reptiles, but it was very fast-moving. It shows numerous characteristics that were once thought to be exclusively dinosaurian.*

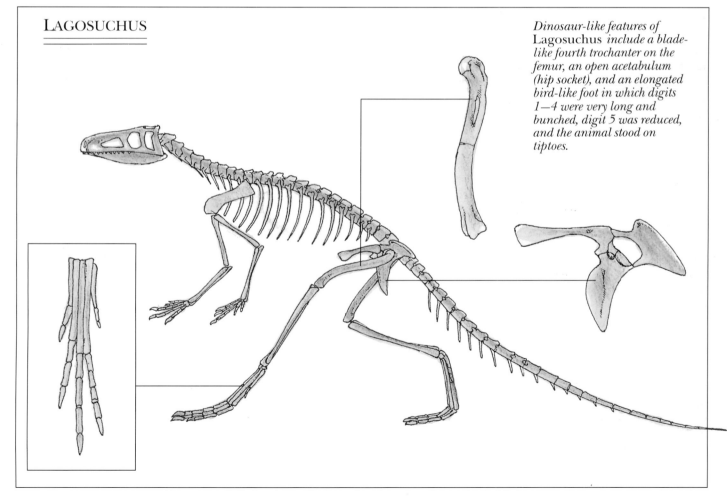

LAGOSUCHUS

Dinosaur-like features of Lagosuchus *include a blade-like fourth trochanter on the femur, an open acetabulum (hip socket), and an elongated bird-like foot in which digits 1—4 were very long and bunched, digit 5 was reduced, and the animal stood on tiptoes.*

toes and the digitigrade posture of the foot, in which only the toes touch the ground, not the sole of the foot as in earlier archosaurs — and in humans today.

Most of the dinosaur-like characters are also seen in the flying pterosaurs. Certain palaeontologists argue that *Lagosuchus*, the pterosaurs, and the dinosaurs together form a major clade that arose in the Middle to Late Triassic, some 230 million years ago.

The dinosaur-like synapomorphies of this clade, and their further modification in the dinosaurs proper, are part of a major series of related anatomical changes that took place among the archosaurs during the Triassic, and which may have been the key to the origin of the dinosaurs.

The origin of the dinosaurs

Most of the synapomorphies of the leg that appear in *Ornithosuchus*, advance in *Lagosuchus*, and come to full development in the dinosaurs are concerned with the acquisition of an erect gait — or the fully upright posture. It is important to note that erect or upright gait does not necessarily mean bipedal. Cows and horses have the erect gait and posture, just as much as humans do.

The first archosaurs were sprawlers, like modern lizards and salamanders. The limbs stuck out sideways from the body, and the elbows and knees form right angles at all times as the animal walks. Even at speed, a lizard generally swings its limbs far out to the side of its body, and it is assumed that the Early Triassic archosaurs moved in a similar way. During the Middle Triassic, most archosaurs adopted a semi-erect posture in which the body could be lifted clear of the ground, with the arms and legs tucked partly underneath for rapid locomotion. Finally, in the Middle and Late Triassic, the two archosaur lineages noted above — the crocodilian and dinosaur lines — adopted an erect posture in which the limbs were tucked underneath the body at all times. This seems to have happened independently in each line.

The aetosaurs, rauisuchians and early crocodilians evolved an erect posture in which the acetabula shifted beneath the hip bones and the heads of the femurs fitted straight up into them, like straight columns beneath a building. The members of the dinosaur line used the approach seen in mammals, in which the acetabula remain on the side of the hip bones but the femurs develop right-angled heads that fit in from the sides. In this design the relationship of hip girdle and leg is more like a buttress on the side of a church building, rather than a column beneath its roof, but the result is the same. The legs of dinosaurs,

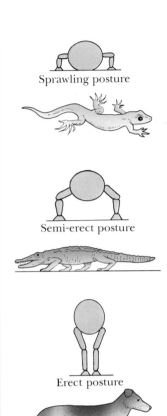

Sprawling posture

Semi-erect posture

Erect posture

The evolution of posture in Triassic archosaurs. Early forms, such as Proterosuchus, *were sprawlers and held their limbs out to the side, as do modern lizards and salamanders. Later archosaurs had a semi-erect posture like* Riojasuchus *and modern crocodiles, in which the body was held clear of the ground during walking. Dinosaurs, as well as their close relatives* Ornithosuchus *and* Lagosuchus, *had a fully erect gait in which the limbs were tucked in, directly beneath the body. The advantages of erect gait are confirmed by the fact that modern birds and modern mammals adopt this posture.*

and of mammals, come together in a slightly knock-kneed fashion beneath the body, and this is a crucial feature.

Advantages of an erect posture

The erect posture of dinosaurs is often said to be the key to their success. Why is this? An important reason is that an erect posture is mechanically more satisfactory than a sprawling one. The weight of the body is supported entirely from below. In a sprawler, the weight of the body is supported from the sides. While gravity effectively pulls straight down from the centre of the body mass, in a sprawler this force has to be converted into a sideways component along the femur or humerus (upper arm bone), and then a vertical component down the tibia and fibula, and the radius and ulna (forearm bones), which causes great stresses on the limb bones and joints. These stresses are avoided if the gravitational force of the animal's mass is transferred down through a straight, erect limb.

This mechanical advantage has several important consequences. Firstly, erect animals can run in a more sustained way: not necessarily faster, but with more stamina, because the effort of supporting the body weight is much less than in a sprawler. This would have been an immediate advantage to an archosaur chasing sprawling prey animals or escaping from a sprawling carnivore. Interestingly, the main plant-eating groups of the Middle Triassic, the pig-like rhynchosaurs and dicynodonts, were evolving semi-erect gaits at the same time. Indeed, the ancestors of the mammals, the cynodonts — which were moderate-sized carnivores at that stage — also showed similar advances.

The "empty ecospace"

Until recently, the success of the dinosaurs over the rhynchosaurs, dicynodonts and cynodonts was explained by a competitive model. It was assumed that the erect gait of the dinosaurs, and other supposed advantages, allowed them to vanquish other Triassic animals and drive them to extinction.

There was a major crisis about 225 million years ago, some five million years after the origin of the first small dinosaurs. Numerous groups of animals died out in the sea and on land, as a result of a great climatic change or some other catastrophe. There is evidence that plants underwent major evolutionary upheavals about this time, and the rhynchosaurs and dicynodonts may have died out when they lost their essential plant foods. Whatever the cause, there was a mass extinction 225 million years ago. A mass extinction is the disappearance of a broad cross-sec-

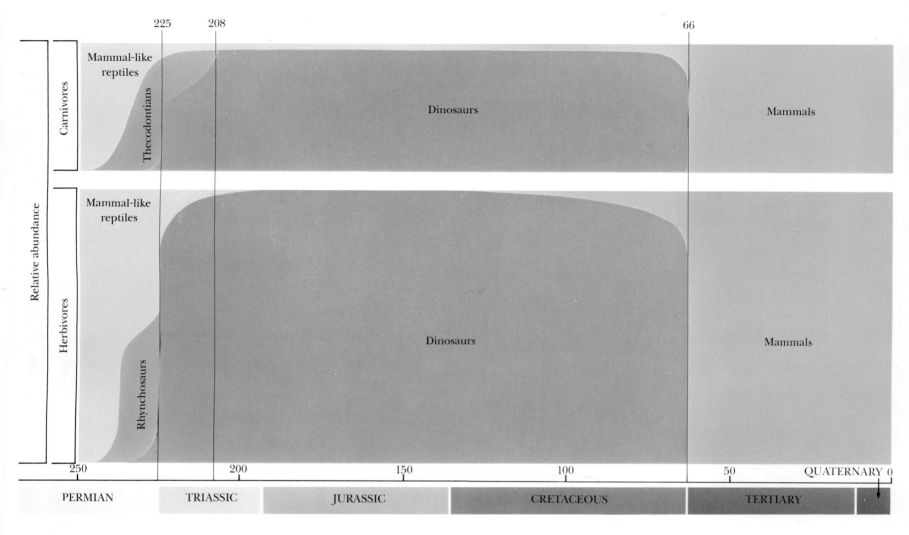

How the mammal-like reptiles, thecodontians and rhynchosaurs were replaced by the dinosaurs in the Late Triassic. The dominant rhynchosaurs, and many of the thecodontians, died out in a mass extinction "event" 225 million years ago. The theropod (carnivorous) dinosaurs and prosauropod (herbivorous) dinosaurs then evolved quickly, taking their opportunities. A second mass extinction, 208 million years ago, saw the end of the thecodontians, and the further rapid evolution of new dinosaur groups.

tion of plant and animal groups in a relatively short time. A dozen or more reptile groups died out then, including several significant ones such as the rhynchosaurs, dicynodonts, aetosaurs, and various carnivorous cynodont and "thecodontian" groups. This left a large number of gaps in the ecology and possible lifestyles of terrestrial plants and animals, giving great opportunities for the surviving groups to take over and fill the gaps. The rare early dinosaurs, never more than one or two per cent of their communities before the mass extinction, blossomed to represent 50 per cent or more within a few million years.

This model for the origin of the dinosaurs — their opportunistic radiation into "empty ecospace" — is very different from the old competitive model. There is no long-term battle, in which whole groups are pitted against each other globally. The dinosaurs were lucky to be around at the right time, and they seized the opportunity. Competitive advantage no doubt played a part, however. The small *Lagosuchus*-like dinosaurs had an effective erect gait, with all of its advantages, and they were agile carnivores able to hunt a variety of prey. Just as the mammals replaced the dinosaurs opportunistically after the latter's extinction, some 160 million years later, so the dinosaurs probably owed 95 per cent of their success to being in the right place at the right time, and five per cent to their competitive attributes.

Why did the mammals not succeed 225 million years ago? Their close ancestors, the cynodonts, were already present on the Earth. The dinosaurs radiated first and achieved large size while the first mammals were no more than mouse-sized. So long as the dinosaurs ruled the Earth, these small early mammals could not overcome them, and mammals did not exceed the size of a cat until the dino-

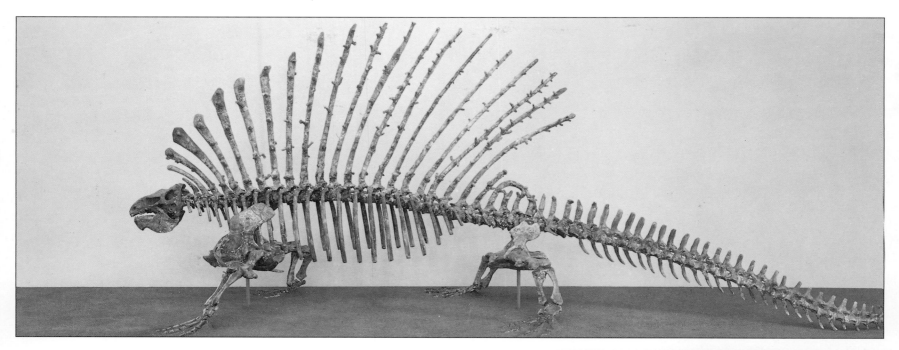

saurs died out.

Immediately after the mass extinction of the dicynodonts, rhynchosaurs, aetosaurs and others, there were a few million years of rapid evolution as new groups radiated into the newly vacated "ecospace". There were openings for plant-eaters of all sizes, and for moderate-sized carnivores to prey on the other surviving animals. The rauisuchians lived on through the mass extinction and were the top carnivores for another 17 million years. A second mass extinction at the end of the Triassic period, 208 million years ago, saw the end of the rauisuchians and phytosaurs (the last of the "thecodontians"), as well as some cynodont and other groups. The dinosaurs, already well established as medium to large herbivores and small to medium carnivores, radiated again, and new specialized plant-eating types as well as larger carnivores came on the scene.

This period of upheaval in the Late Triassic, punctuated by two mass extinctions, saw not only the two-phase radiation of the dinosaurs to a position of dominance on land, but also the radiation of other important vertebrate groups (animals with backbones). The first turtles, sphenodontians (lizard-like animals), pterosaurs, crocodilians and mammals all date from this time. Indeed, on a broader scale, this episode in the long history of vertebrate evolution marks a major transition between the older groups and the appearance of many newer groups that are still with us today.

(Cont page 28.)

The skeleton of the sail-backed, mammal-like reptile Edaphosaurus *(above) from the Early Permian of Texas. The mammal-like reptiles ruled the Earth for some 100 million years before the dinosaurs came on the scene. The "sail" was covered with skin and probably helped in temperature control.*

The head of a sail-back, Dimetrodon *(right), related to* Edaphosaurus *but obviously a carnivore, as shown by the teeth.* Dimetrodon *probably fed on the herbivorous* Edaphosaurus.

THE GEOLOGICAL TIME SCALE

The geological time scale is an internationally agreed standard that has been established over the past 200 years. It is based on numerous independent studies of fossils, regional geology in all parts of the world and exact age dating using a variety of radiometric techniques. The vastness of time is shown by the fact that humans have been around for only the last 0.1 per cent of the age of the earth.

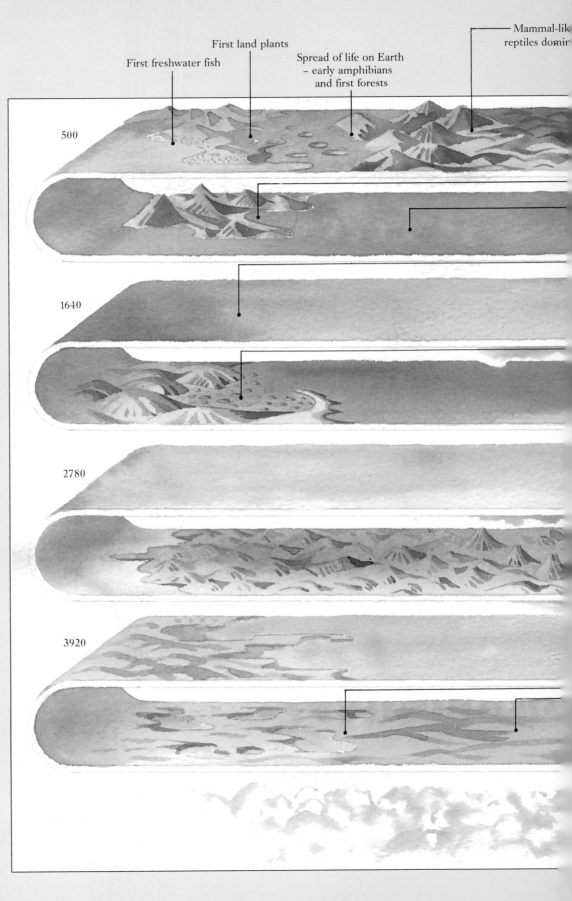

First freshwater fish

First land plants

Spread of life on Earth – early amphibians and first forests

Mammal-lik reptiles domin

500

1640

2780

3920

MILLION YEARS AGO		
0	QUATERNARY	*The last 66 million years, the age of the mammals, record the radiation of the familiar modern groups such as mice, bats, horses, monkeys, elephants, whales and humans.*
	TERTIARY	
66		
70	CRETACEOUS	*The Cretaceous period saw the heyday of many dinosaur groups, such as the giant tyrannosaurs, the armoured ankylosaurs and ceratopsians, and the herbivorous ornithopods. All these groups died out in the last 5 million years or so of the period, between 61 and 66 million years ago.*
80		
90		
100		
110		
120		
130		
140		
150	JURASSIC	*Major dinosaur groups in the Jurassic included the carnivorous megalosaurs and allosaurs, the giant herbivorous sauropods and the plated stegosaurs. Smaller carnivores gave rise to the birds at the end of the Jurassic.*
160		
170		
180		
190		
200		*The Triassic period opened with a world dominated by mammal-like reptiles and other primitive forms. Most of these were wiped out in the Late Triassic by two mass extinctions.*
210	TRIASSIC	
220		

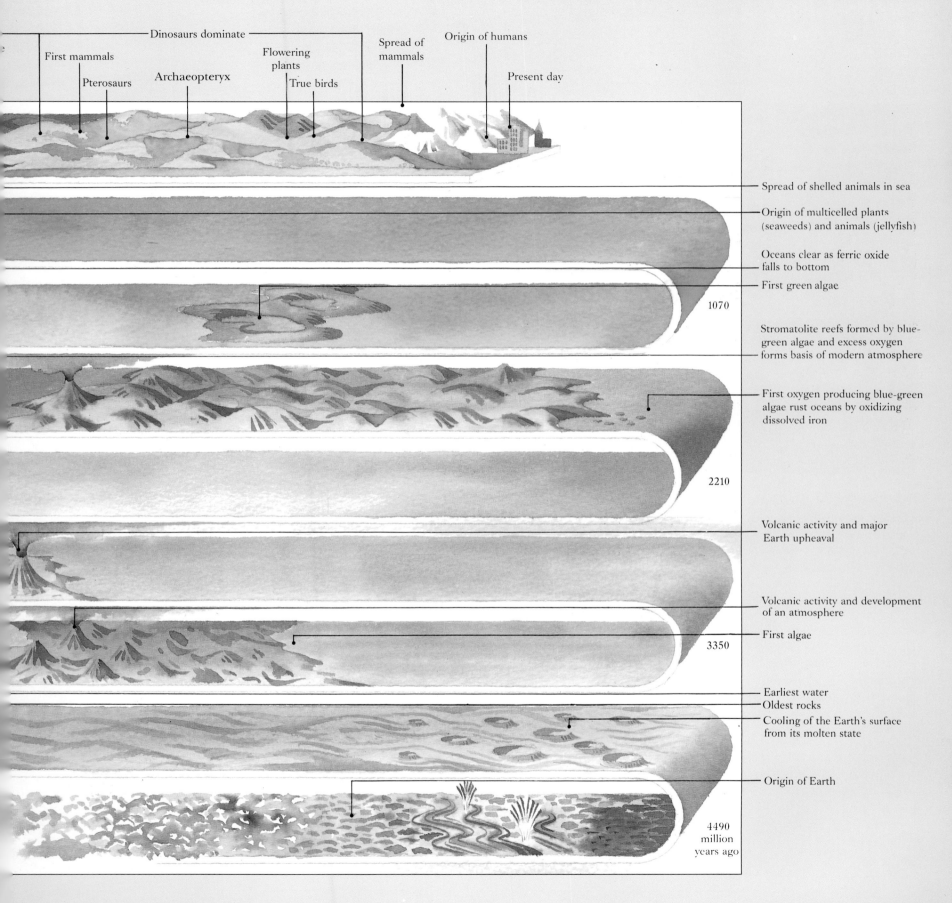

First mammals

Pterosaurs

Dinosaurs dominate

Archaeopteryx

Flowering plants

True birds

Spread of mammals

Origin of humans

Present day

Spread of shelled animals in sea

Origin of multicelled plants (seaweeds) and animals (jellyfish)

Oceans clear as ferric oxide falls to bottom

First green algae

1070

Stromatolite reefs formed by blue-green algae and excess oxygen forms basis of modern atmosphere

First oxygen producing blue-green algae rust oceans by oxidizing dissolved iron

2210

Volcanic activity and major Earth upheaval

Volcanic activity and development of an atmosphere

First algae

3350

Earliest water

Oldest rocks

Cooling of the Earth's surface from its molten state

Origin of Earth

4490 million years ago

27

The history of life

The Earth is reckoned to be about 4,600 million years old. For the first 1,000 million years or so of its history, we have no evidence for life of any kind. Conditions on the Earth were quite unsuitable for life initially: the surface was molten at first, and volcanoes sent out clouds of poisonous gas and floods of lava and explosive debris. There were no oceans and there was no atmosphere.

The first evidence for life dates back to 3,500 million years ago, when fossils of algal mounds called stromatolites first appear in the geological record. Stromatolites are still found today, built up from thin layers of blue-green algae and trapped mud. (Blue-green algae are among the simplest living organisms, being single-celled and lacking a nucleus or cellular control centre.) The first fossils in which cell shapes can be seen are preserved in chert rocks dated at around 3,100 million years old. The only living things on the Earth for many hundreds of millions of years were microscopic organisms such as these blue-green algae, and also bacteria.

More complex single-celled organisms arose some 1,000 million years ago. These had a nucleus and other specialized organelles within each cell. Multi-celled plants and animals came on the scene some 700 million years ago.

Fucus vesiculosus (above), a common seaweed on European beaches. This simple plant, a many-celled alga, feeds on nutrients in sea water drawn through its fronds; it is distantly related, like all living things, to the first single-celled forms of life on Earth.

These may have looked rather like seaweeds, sponges and jellyfish. More complex animal groups arose relatively rapidly 570 million years ago, when the first skeletonized forms are found as fossils. They include brachiopods and molluscs with their limy shells, arthropods with their mobile external skeletons, and a little later, corals, sea urchins, and the first fish.

The appearance of skeletonized animals is taken to mark a major division in the geological time scale. This time scale is an international standard, set up initially in the early 19th century to divide the history of the Earth into manageable units. The boundaries between the units usually coincide with some major event in the history of life, so that the first 4,000 million years of Earth's history is termed the Precambrian, and the last 570 million years is the Phanerozoic, meaning "abundant life". The appearance of skeletonized animals marks the boundary.

The Phanerozoic, although only one-eighth of the known history of the Earth, has been most studied because many phases of our own evolution can be detected during this time, and because the record of the rocks generally improves towards the present day. Whereas the Precambrian cannot easily be subdivided into smaller time units, the Phanerozoic has been, and particularly for its last 100 million years. The science of establishing and understanding geological time, stratigraphy, is now very advanced (see below).

The Phanerozoic is divided into three main eras: the Palaeozoic ("ancient life"), from 570 to 245 million years ago, the Mesozoic ("middle life"), from 245 to 66 million years ago, and the Cenozoic ("recent life") for the last 66 million years. The dinosaurs ruled the Earth during the Mesozoic, and indeed the Mesozoic/Cenozoic boundary is precisely marked by their disappearance. The vertebrates arose some 520 million years ago; the first forms were primitive fish. At that time, life was almost entirely restricted to the sea. Various plants and animals ventured into fresh waters, and then onto land about 420 million years ago. The first vertebrates to exploit the land were amphibians, which appeared 370 million years ago.

The Mesozoic Era is divided into three periods: the Triassic (245-208 million years ago), the Jurassic (208-144) and the Cretaceous (144-66). The Triassic followed a mass extinction at the end of the Palaeozoic Era, and this may have permitted the initial radiation of the thecodontians, rhynchosaurs and others. As we have seen, the dinosaurs and many other important groups arose in the Late Triassic, while the mass extinction at the Triassic/Jurassic boundary marked the second phase of dinosaur radiation.

The geological time scale. This standard international reference scale is based on close study of the sequence of rocks worldwide and the fossils they contain. The named periods of geological time are separated by major events of various kinds that act as important markers. The exact dates, in millions of years, have been determined by independent geochemical tests based on natural radioactivity.

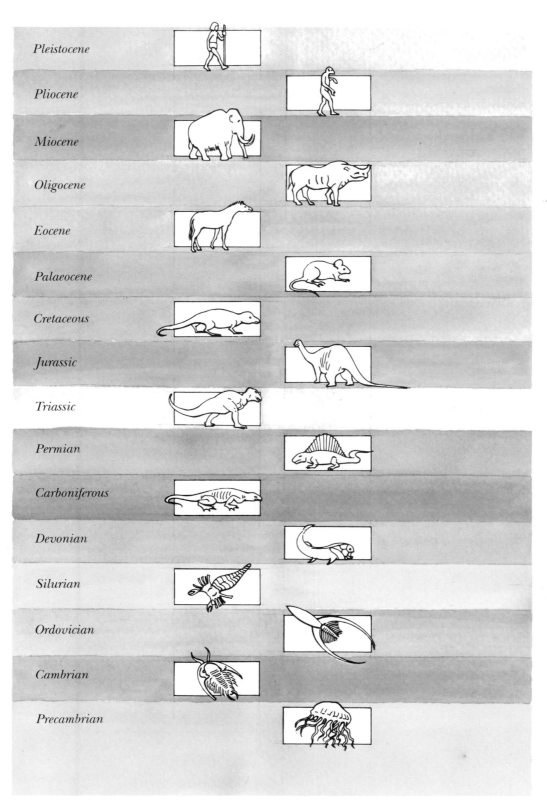

Pleistocene — First modern humans appear; the Great Ice Ages; mammoths.

Pliocene — First humans appear; most modern plants and animals.

Miocene — Spread of great grasslands; rise of cattle and deer.

Oligocene — First rhinos, pigs, monkeys, squirrels, deer.

Eocene — First elephants, horses, bats, rabbits, camels, ducks.

Palaeocene — Beginning of age of mammals; first hedgehogs, owls.

Cretaceous — First modern mammals; last dinosaurs, pterosaurs, etc.

Jurassic — Height of the age of the dinosaurs; first birds.

Triassic — Origin of the dinosaurs; first mammals, crocodiles, frogs.

Permian — Age of mammal-like reptiles; one supercontinent.

Carboniferous — The coal age; amphibians rule the earth; first reptiles.

Devonian — The age of fishes; first sharks and bony fishes.

Silurian — First land plants; giant sea scorpions.

Ordovician — First corals and star fish; trilobites and graptolites.

Cambrian — Radiation of life in the sea: first shelled animals.

Precambrian — Origin of the earth; origin of life; origin of complex life.

Measuring geological time

The geological time scale is an international standard, first set up 180 years ago. Over the years it has been refined, but the broad outlines remain since they were based on major upheavals or changes in the history of the Earth and of life, such as mass extinctions. The geological time scale is based on an understanding of two aspects of the past: relative time and absolute time.

The divisions of the geological column are based on relative dating. The first geologists (scientists who study rocks and the history of the Earth) noticed that different fossils often seemed to be found together in repeated assemblages, and that there was some kind of sequence to these assemblages. For example, fossils A, B and C were always found together in the same layer or rock, and always below fossils X, Y and Z. These observations led to two conclusions. Firstly, in layered rocks, the oldest rocks are at the bottom of the pile and the youngest at the top (the "layer

Sedimentary rocks such as mudstones, sandstones and limestones are deposited in layers (beds or strata). The oldest beds are at the bottom, the youngest at the top. Later, these simple layers may be modified by massive forces in the Earth's crust. The crust may crack into separate blocks and faults may cause blocks to drop (1) or move sideways (2,3). Molten rocks may be injected from deep below, often in the form of a vertical dyke.

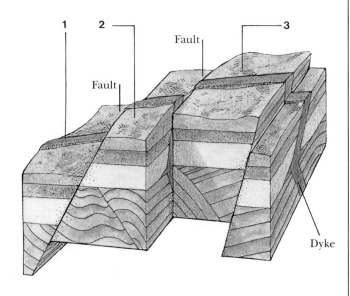

cake" principle). Relative ages can therefore be established in one place, or from place to place.

The second principle which was firmly established is correlation by means of fossils. The fossil assemblage A-B-C represents a finite unit of geological time, and whenever those fossils are found together, the geologist has identified rocks laid down at only that time — even if one sample comes from Alaska and the other from China. The sequence and divisions of geological time into eras, periods, and smaller units called stages, substages, and zones, are based on these two principles. In parts of the column, stages are only one million years or less, so that the techniques allow considerable precision.

These techniques do not give you precise ages — that is, the absolute dates in terms of millions of years. How have geologists established with some confidence that the Triassic, for example, lasted from 245 to 208 million years ago, plus or minus an error of one to three per cent? These absolute dates are determined by radiometric dating. As a rock

The "badlands" of southern Alberta (above). Rivers cut through the dinosaur-rich sediments and expose fresh fossils every year.

A quarry in the Middle Jurassic of Oxfordshire, site of isolated dinosaur fossils (left). Note the layering in the limy mudstone.

forms, certain of the physical elements, such as uranium, thorium or potassium, may be encapsulated within it in an unstable condition. Over time, these elements "decay", giving off radioactivity, and turning into another elemental form as they do so. For instance, uranium-238 becomes lead-206, thorium-232 becomes lead-208, and potassium-40 becomes argon-40.

These transitions have measurable half-lives, that is the time it takes for half of the original element to decay. In the above examples the half-lives are 4,510 Myr (million years), 13,900 Myr and 1300 Myr respectively. If the proportions of, say, potassium-40 to argon-40 can be measured in a rock sample then the exact age of formation of that rock can be calculated. Of course, the technique is much more complex than described here, but dates measured using different "decay pairs" often give very good agreement about the absolute age of a rock sample. The main problem is that only certain kinds of rocks, such as lavas, can be dated radiometrically.

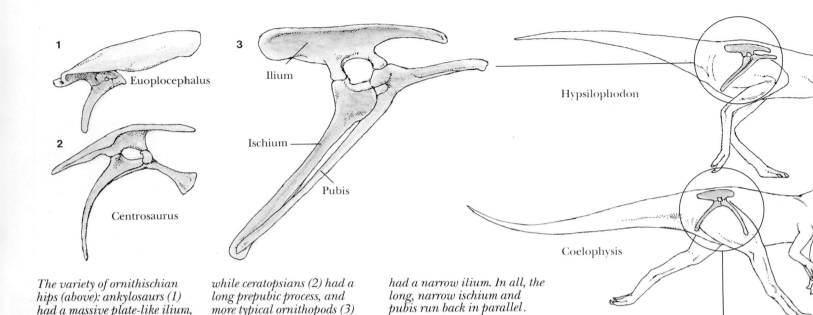

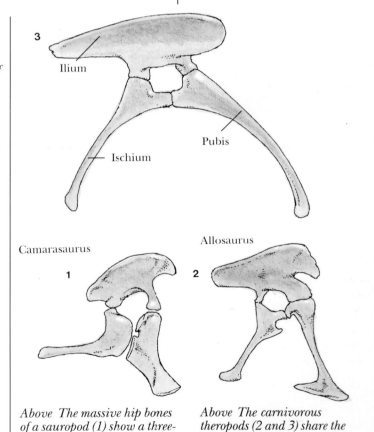

The variety of ornithischian hips (above): ankylosaurs (1) had a massive plate-like ilium, while ceratopsians (2) had a long prepubic process, and more typical ornithopods (3) had a narrow ilium. In all, the long, narrow ischium and pubis run back in parallel.

The diversity of the dinosaurs

In the past 170 years since the first dinosaur was named, palaeontologists have recorded 1,000 or more species. Each species is placed in a larger group, the genus, which may be composed of several species. Each genus and species has a scientific name, generally composed of Greek or Latin words, and that scientific name is always presented in *italics* (or underlined). The generic name starts with a capital letter, the specific name has lower-case letters. Thus, *Tyrannosaurus rex* is the species *rex* of the genus *Tyrannosaurus*; there may be other species in that genus.

The 1,000 or so dinosaur species fall into about 400 genera. These in turn are classified into families, infra-orders, and suborders, depending upon how they appear to be related — and that is established by cladistic analysis. A familiar modern example may help to explain these "tax-onomic" terms, that is, terms used in classification. All domestic dogs belong to the species *Canis familiaris*, meaning "common dog". The wolf is another species of the same genus, *Canis lupus*. The genus *Canis* is a member of the family *Canidae*, together with the foxes, genus *Vulpes*, the Arctic fox, *Alopex*, and others. The family *Canidae*, dogs in general, is in turn a member of the infraorder *Canoidea*, together with the bears, of the suborder *Fissipedia*, and of the order *Carnivora*, along with cats, weasels and seals.

The phylogeny of the dinosaurs, as established from cladistic analysis shows the diversity of the group and how new families kept appearing throughout their 160-million-year tenure on this planet. The phylogeny may be interpreted in the form of a classification (see opposite).

The basic division of the order Dinosauria into the suborders Ornithischia and Saurischia is based on the general patterns of their hip bones. Saurischians have the "lizard hip", the primitive pattern seen in all other reptiles; the two lower bony elements of the hip, the pubis and ischium, run in opposite directions. The ornithischians have the "bird-hip" in which the pubis has swung back to run parallel to the ischium. A secondary prepubic process, pointing forwards, may also be present. Oddly, the ornithischian hip is not seen in birds: the latter are saurischians that independently evolved a similar hip pattern.

Above The massive hip bones of a sauropod (1) show a three-rayed pattern, with the pubis and ischium projecting in separate directions.

Above The carnivorous theropods (2 and 3) share the saurischian hip pattern of sauropods. The pubis has a characteristic "foot" at the bottom.

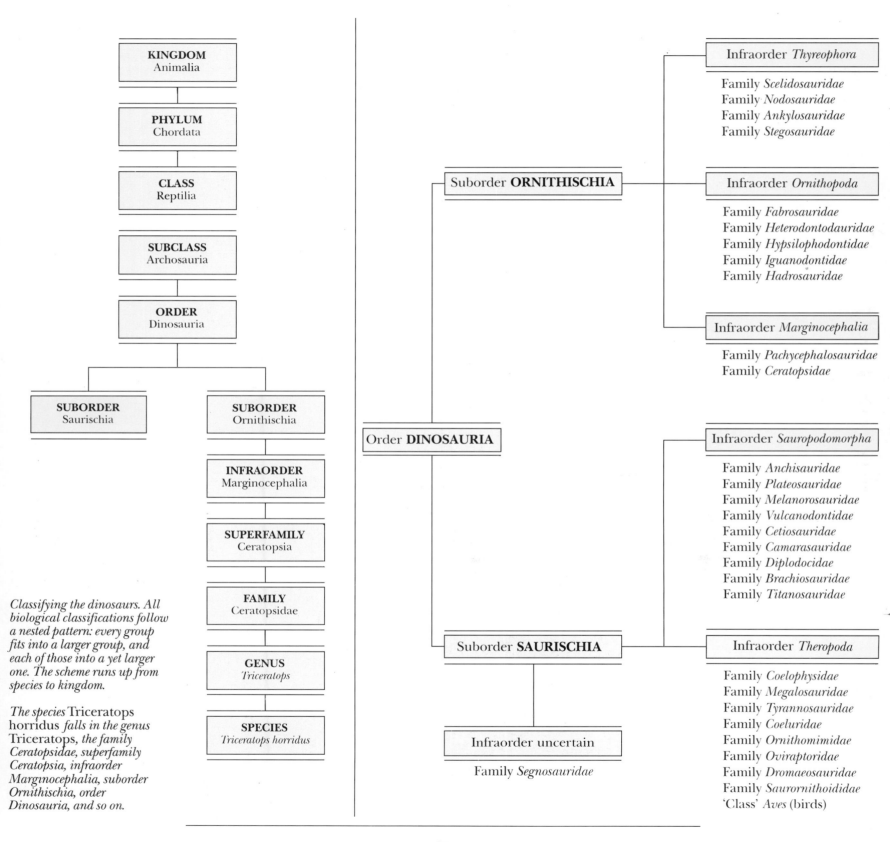

KINGDOM
Animalia

PHYLUM
Chordata

CLASS
Reptilia

SUBCLASS
Archosauria

ORDER
Dinosauria

SUBORDER
Saurischia

SUBORDER
Ornithischia

INFRAORDER
Marginocephalia

SUPERFAMILY
Ceratopsia

FAMILY
Ceratopsidae

GENUS
Triceratops

SPECIES
Triceratops horridus

Classifying the dinosaurs. All biological classifications follow a nested pattern: every group fits into a larger group, and each of those into a yet larger one. The scheme runs up from species to kingdom.

The species Triceratops horridus *falls in the genus* Triceratops, *the family Ceratopsidae, superfamily Ceratopsia, infraorder Marginocephalia, suborder Ornithischia, order Dinosauria, and so on.*

Order **DINOSAURIA**

Suborder **ORNITHISCHIA**

Infraorder *Thyreophora*

Family *Scelidosauridae*
Family *Nodosauridae*
Family *Ankylosauridae*
Family *Stegosauridae*

Infraorder *Ornithopoda*

Family *Fabrosauridae*
Family *Heterodontodauridae*
Family *Hypsilophodontidae*
Family *Iguanodontidae*
Family *Hadrosauridae*

Infraorder *Marginocephalia*

Family *Pachycephalosauridae*
Family *Ceratopsidae*

Suborder **SAURISCHIA**

Infraorder *Sauropodomorpha*

Family *Anchisauridae*
Family *Plateosauridae*
Family *Melanorosauridae*
Family *Vulcanodontidae*
Family *Cetiosauridae*
Family *Camarasauridae*
Family *Diplodocidae*
Family *Brachiosauridae*
Family *Titanosauridae*

Infraorder *Theropoda*

Family *Coelophysidae*
Family *Megalosauridae*
Family *Tyrannosauridae*
Family *Coeluridae*
Family *Ornithomimidae*
Family *Oviraptoridae*
Family *Dromaeosauridae*
Family *Saurornithoididae*
'Class' *Aves* (birds)

Infraorder uncertain

Family *Segnosauridae*

DINOSAURS OF THE LATE TRIASSIC

The first dinosaurs in the Late Triassic of Europe and North America, were small or medium-sized predatory theropods, such as *Procompsognathus* and *Halticosaurus* in this scene from southern Germany. The main herbivores were the larger sauropods such as *Plateosaurus*.

The Triassic world was a single supercontinent, Pangaea, and dinosaurs could walk to any part of the globe over dry land. Climates were warm, and forests subtropical, dominated by tree-like cycads, clubmosses and conifers, as well as low ferns and horsetails. Other animals in the scene include the first mammal to walk the Earth, *Morganucodon* (top left), the first pterosaur *Eudimorphodon* (top centre), a gliding "lizard", *Kuehneosaurus* (top right), the first crocodilian *Protosuchus* (centre), and the first sphenodontid *Planocephalosaurus*.

How the world looked in this period

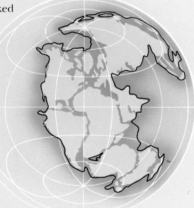

The three dinosaurs from the Late Triassic of Germany are the small predator Procompsognathus *(1), which fed on the early mammals and sphenodontids, its larger relative* Halticosaurus *(2), which may have preyed on larger animals, and the well-known herbivore* Plateosaurus *(3). This was the first "large" dinosaur, being up to eight metres long, a giant by human standards.*

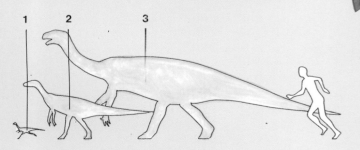

CHAPTER TWO

DINOSAURS IN THE FIELD

Dinosaur fossils come in many shapes and sizes. The most obvious are single bones or whole skeletons, which may be preserved by fossilization with as much detail as they had in life. There are many other kinds of dinosaur fossils. These include footprints, which are often found in great abundance and can tell us a great deal about dinosaurian behaviour. Rarer fossils include impressions of the skin of mummified dinosaurs, eggs, nests and stomach stones, all of which offer special information on the lifestyles of their owners.

Dinosaur bones and teeth

The commonest dinosaur remains on display in the museums of the world are bones and teeth. These are the so-called "hard parts" of an animal, that is, partially mineralized portions that are resistant to the normal processes of decomposition which attack and rot away the "soft parts" of an animal carcass.

Bones and teeth are made from related biological materials, being composed of a mixture of flexible, fibrous tissues that give them strength, and hard non-living minerals (principally apatite, a form of calcium phosphate) that give them hardness. Bone consists of a mesh of long, flexible fibres of collagen, a protein, upon which thin slivers of apatite have crystallized. In life it contains living cells, osteocytes, that make new bone and maintain the existing bone's structure. There are canals of various sizes within the fabric of bone tissue and these provide passageways for blood ves-

A tooth of the carnivorous dinosaur Megalosaurus, *showing the characteristic curved shape and serrated edges (above).*

The massive limb bones of a sauropod as they were found in the field (right). The bones have been cleared of rock, but they need careful handling.

sels and nerves. Hence, bone is in no way a dead tissue: throughout the life of an animal, it grows, is maintained and remodelled just like any other part of the body.

Bones have the obvious functions of supporting the softer parts of the body and providing the firm attachment sites needed for the operation of muscles and ligaments. In addition, bones act as a mineral store — a source of phosphate, for example, which is needed for energy conversion. Phosphate is maintained at the correct level in the blood by constant exchange with the bones; apatite may be deposited in bone to lower phosphate levels in the blood, while phosphate can be extracted from the bone to raise blood levels, leaving great secondary channels eaten into the primary structure.

Teeth consist of several tissue types. The bulk of a tooth is made from dentine, a relatively soft form of apatite and collagen that contains narrow tubules. The upper part of the tooth, the crown, is covered with a cap of enamel. This is an inert, crystalline layer of apatite that is formed before eruption of the tooth and cannot be remodelled. Dentine, on the other hand, is a living tissue like bone, and it is supplied by nerves and blood vessels that enter the pulp cavity in the root of the tooth.

Bones and teeth are already partially mineralized in life, and they may then be readily fossilized after death. At some stage in the long process of fossilization, the living portions of teeth and bones are generally lost by decomposition: the blood vessels, nerves and osteocytes rot away, and the collagen fibres are replaced by a hard mineral. However, the pattern of the internal structure may be little affected by this, and cross-sections of fossil bones and teeth can show

virtually as much detail as those of fresh ones. The cavities are generally filled with mineral deposits of some kind or another, but these often serve to preserve even microscopic details very beautifully.

Processes of fossilization

A fairly predictable sequence of events leads to the formation of a dinosaur (or any other) fossil. At each step along the way, both specimens and information are lost. In other words, every dinosaur that ever lived will not be found as a fossil, because many individual specimens are lost at each stage between the living dinosaurs themselves and the discovery of their fossils. In addition, information on dinosaurian anatomy is lost, step-by-step, from the death of the animal to its eventual discovery and presentation in a museum exhibit. In fact, the odds are very much stacked against a particular dinosaur being preserved as a fossil, and against that preservation showing us all of the details of its anatomy. Yet thousands of dinosaur fossils have been collected over the years. This illustrates the fact that many billions or trillions of individual dinosaurs walked the surface of the Earth. Even if only 0.001 per cent of them ever turn up as fossilized skeletons, we can expect to find thousands more fossils.

Let us follow some of the events that may happen after a dinosaur dies. Its body might have lain on the dry land where scavengers — other dinosaurs, mammals, lizards — would have stripped the flesh from its bones. Smaller organisms then removed every vestige of soft tissue, and some bacteria could have started breaking down the bones as well. In most cases, the skeleton would eventually disintegrate to nothing under the combined attack of scavengers, decomposers and the elements.

Occasionally, the carcass might have ended up in a pond or a river. In these cases, the scavengers may have been fish and crocodilians, but the stripping-down job would be just as efficient as on land. However, the bones would be more likely to be buried under mud and sand in the bottom of the pond, or on the inside bend of a river, where deposition takes place. This would prevent total decomposition, and might even keep some of the bones joined together.

Rivers would tend to transport the carcass some distance, depending on its size and the force of the current. Cases are known, such as in the Tendaguru of Tanzania, where large sauropod dinosaurs have been found missing their heads and feet. It seems that, once the flesh was removed, the skull flopped about at the end of the long neck bones until it was caught up by a modest current, sep-

As the carcass of an animal decomposes, soft tissues generally soon disappear to scavengers and bacteria. The hard parts — bones — are usually left undamaged, for a time. The skeleton tends to disintegrate eventually if left exposed to the air, but it may be buried under layers of mud or sand, under water (below) or in a desert.

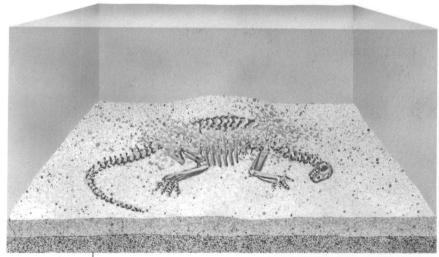

The bones are covered in sediment preventing them from becoming eroded (above).

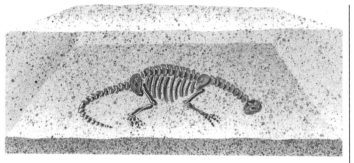

As sediment builds up (left) the buried bones are subject to various changes in the rock. The spaces in the bone may become "permineralized" as minerals in water solution infiltrate and solidify. Or, the bony tissue itself is replaced, crystal by crystal, by another hard mineral; the structure is then entirely petrified, or "turned to stone".

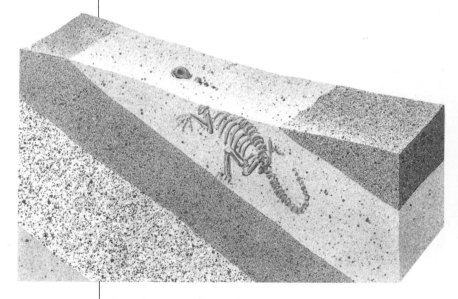

Over the course of time, the rocks may be uplifted or tilted by movements in the Earth's crust. Erosion may expose the ancient sediments and the fossilized bones they contain (above).

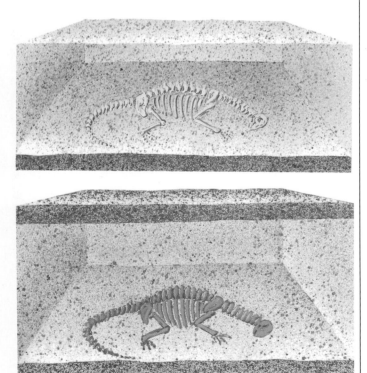

Occasionally the bones dissolve but leave a cast which, with time, fills with minerals, resulting in a skeletal replica (left).

arated and swept away. The lack of feet may be because the animal died in a standing posture, and its body weight drove the feet into the bottom sediments, where they were held fast even after the flesh had rotted; currents, meanwhile, rolled the rest of the skeleton away.

The bottoms of some lakes are anoxic (lacking oxygen) and can support little life other than certain bacteria that consume sulphur instead of oxygen. In these cases, any carcasses that fall into the anoxic bottom waters may be "pickled" and protected from scavenging. The skeletons are preserved complete and in articulation (with bones connected to each other). Smaller animals such as fish that fall into these anoxic muds may be nearly perfectly preserved, with their skins and internal organs represented as shadows on the fine mudstone to which the mud eventually turns. This is rarely the case for dinosaurs, unfortunately.

The dinosaur beds of southern Alberta. The Late Cretaceous sandstones and mudstones, 70 million years old, are being eroded today by wind and rain, and large numbers of dinosaur bones are exposed on the flat surface in the foreground (above).

After a dinosaur carcass has survived scavenging, decomposition and transport by wind or water (these processes probably prevented 99.99 per cent of dinosaurs from even becoming candidates for preservation), the processes of burial and fossilization begin. Should the skeleton end up in an area of sediment deposition, such as a lake bed, delta mouth, sand bar or sand-dune field, it may be buried rapidly beneath the sand or mud. Under certain conditions sediment may be deposited fast enough to bury the skeleton several metres deep within a few years.

As sediment piles up above, its weight produces high pressures underground, which force out water contained in the pore spaces and cause cementation of the loose sand or mud grains. Individual grains may recrystallize under pressure, or water rich in dissolved minerals might deposit its minerals out of solution as a "cement". In both cases,

The original rock layers are highlighted by the brown horizon. Erosion has worn deep runnels in the mudstone, and a piece of bone is exposed on a natural pillar (left).

The jawbone of a hadrosaur (a duckbilled dinosaur) as found by a bone prospector in southern Alberta. The specimen shows the multiple rows of teeth on the inside of the lower jaw (right).

The skull cap of an ankylosaur (left), an armoured plant-eating dinosaur, eroded out of the rock in the "badlands" by two or three years of water and wind action.

loose sediments become sedimentary rocks such as mudstone, sandstone or limestone. The pressure and mineral-rich water affect the entombed bones and teeth as well, and pore spaces within them tend to fill with minerals such as calcite (calcium carbonate) or iron oxide. This is the process of petrifaction ("turning to rock"), and it is the reason why fossil bones are much heavier than fresh bones.

Numerous dinosaur skeletons must have been lost during the processes of burial and fossilization. If the pore waters were slightly acidic, as in a peaty area, the apatite of the bones and teeth might be dissolved away. In other cases, where burial is very deep or major earth disturbances take place close by, the rocks may be compressed or heated sufficiently to distort or destroy the fossils. Upheavals in the Earth's crust, such as earthquakes and volcanoes, must destroy countless fossils.

The underside of the skull of a ceratopsian (right) — a horned plant-eating dinosaur. One horn is on the left, and the occipital condyle, the ball of bone by which the skull joins to the neck, is on the lower right.

Dinosaur footprints are common, and often large, fossils. It takes a wheelbarrow to move the cast of a single Megalosaurus *print (above). A double set of* Megalosaurus *tracks shows the three great toes on each foot, as two of these animals walked side by side across an ancient shore (right).*

The final stages in the chain from living dinosaur to the discovery of its fossils involve further unlikely circumstances. The body of sedimentary rock that contains the fossils must be lifted to the surface of the Earth, where it can be worn away by erosion. In other words, what was once an area of sedimentary deposition, usually under water, has to be lifted, often into mountains, where the wind, rain and flowing water strip off rock grains. Erosion by the beating sea or by flash floods in the "badlands" may be as rapid as 10-20 centimetres annually, which produces entirely new exposures for geologists to examine every year. Of course, most dinosaur skeletons exposed by erosion probably disintegrate before a collector or scientist chances upon them, so that there is important loss of specimens and information even at this late stage.

Dinosaur footprints

The second-commonest category of dinosaurian fossil consists of footprints, either in isolation or, more usually, in the form of trackways. These are termed "trace fossils" since they represent traces of the activity of dinosaurs, as

Footprints are important fossils since they show the shape of the flesh of the feet, as well as the imprints of the bones and sometimes the claws, and also the exact placing of the feet. These 220-million-year-old tracks from Australia (right) were made by a labyrinthodont, a heavyweight amphibian that lived at the beginning of the age of dinosaurs.

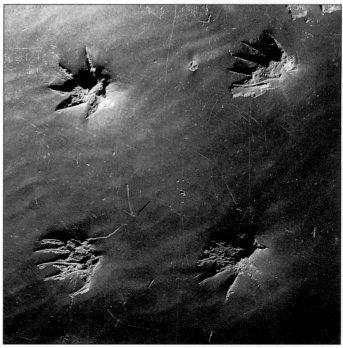

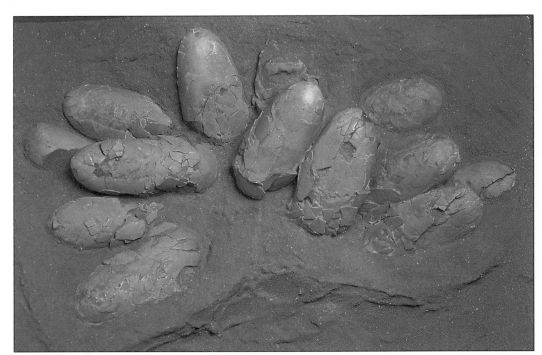

A nest of 13 cylindrical eggs (left) laid by Protoceratops, an early horned dinosaur, in the Middle Cretaceous of Mongolia. The eggs have their calcareous shells preserved, and these show some similarities to the shells of a bird. The eggs were laid upright, with the narrow end of each downwards, and in several concentric circles, of which two are preserved here.

opposed to "body fossils" that contain bones, teeth and other substances of the animal's body. The distinction between body fossils and trace fossils applies to all other kinds of fossils: preserved leaves, tree trunks, shells and insect cuticles are body fossils, while worm tracks, sea urchin burrows and droppings (coprolites) are trace fossils.

Dinosaur trackways are known from numerous localities and from all ages of rocks during the Mesozoic. In many cases, abundant trackways are found in geological formations that lack fossil bones, so they provide useful information on dinosaurian distributions. The trackways can also be identified fairly readily. Each major dinosaur group had differently shaped hands and feet, and these produced characteristic track shapes. The exact species that made a particular footprint cannot usually be identified with certainty, but it is generally possible to pinpoint the family or genus. Another value of dinosaur trackways, and probably the most important, is that they give unique information on several aspects of the creatures' biology and behaviour.

Coprolites are the other main kind of dinosaurian trace fossil. Similarly, they give information of a distributional nature; in the absence of skeletons, they can tell us that dinosaurs were there. They also give clues on diets, since they can be dissected to reveal their contents: leaves, stalks and seeds for herbivores, or broken bones and teeth in the case of carnivores. The plant or animal remains in coprolites can often be identified to species level, and the dinosaur's recent diet precisely analysed.

A hadrosaur egg from the Late Cretaceous of Montana (above). The narrow end was embedded in the sand when it was laid, and the young animal would have hatched through the top.

Skin, eggs and nests

Dinosaurian soft parts are very rare in the fossil record. However, some fossils give us strong hints of a variety of soft structures. The commonest are those that attach directly to the bones, for example cartilages, tendons and muscles. Cartilage is a flexible material closely associated with bone, particularly in young animals as a "precursor", or "blueprint" of the future, fully developed bones.

For instance, the bones of a juvenile dinosaur may show evidence of cartilage at the ends, and hence give clues to the age of the animal at death. Tendons are flexible, fleshy strips of connective tissue that attach muscles to bones. They send fibres deep into the fabric of a bone in order to provide firm anchor, and the locations of these fibrous invaders may be seen under the microscope in a cross-section of the bone. Muscles themselves may be attached directly to the bone over broad patches, where the force is not great enough to require a separate tendon. These various attachment sites leave characteristic patches and processes (knobs) on the surface of the bone, that allow tentative reconstructions of the muscles.

The scales of reptiles, the beaks and feathers of birds, and the nails, claws and hair of mammals are made from the flexible protein keratin. This is essentially a dead tissue once it has formed, which is why it does not hurt to cut your hair or nails. Dinosaurs had a number of keratinous structures, such as claws, scales and beaks. Certain plant-eaters, the duckbills in particular, had horny, keratinous beaks that fitted over the snout bones like the beak of a bird or turtle. Keratin is fossilized only in extremely rare cases, but in some excellently preserved specimens can be quite clearly seen an impression showing the full shape of a horny claw cover or beak.

Internal casts of bones may offer a great deal of unexpected information. For example, the braincase of a typical dinosaur was a relatively small, complex box of bone within the obvious outer box of the skull. Imagine the head skeleton of a dinosaur as an outer shoe box, with a cigarette box inside that contained the brain! The braincase fitted tightly around most of the brain and the cranial nerves that connected to the sensory organs. A cast of the inside of the braincase bones made in flexible plastic or rubber can show the exact shape and size of all parts of the dinosaur brain, and allow serious speculation on its senses and level of intelligence.

Skin impressions of dinosaurs are rare, except in the case of the ankylosaurs, plant-eaters which were covered with a carapace of closely fitting bony lumps or "nodules" within their skin layer. The famous mummified hadrosaurs from the Cretaceous rocks of Canada show impressions of the skin of non-armoured plant-eaters. It is assumed that the carcasses were dried rapidly by the sun; the body juices were removed within a matter of hours or days; and the whole leathery carcass was then buried before it could be scavenged. This fossilization process happens today to the bodies of cattle and camels in the dry parts of Africa and Asia. The fossils so formed show impressions of the skin and parts of the flesh.

Dinosaur eggs and nests have now been found in various geological formations, but they are commonest in the Late Cretaceous deposits of southern France, India and midwestern North America. The reasons for their rarity in the Triassic and Jurassic are unknown. In most respects, the structure of the dinosaurian eggshell is very like that of a bird's egg. Dinosaur eggs vary in form from spherical to thin and almost cigar-shaped, and the largest examples are 30 centimetres long. Eggs have been found on their own and also in specific arrangements that suggest controlled nest-building and egg-laying by the parents. The eggs sometimes contain embryos and they may give other information on dinosaurian reproduction and parental behaviour (see page 117).

An impression of the skin of Scolosaurus *(right), showing the small, irregular bony plates and the larger bosses set into the back. This kind of armour is more easily fossilized than the more typical unarmoured skin of most dinosaurs.*

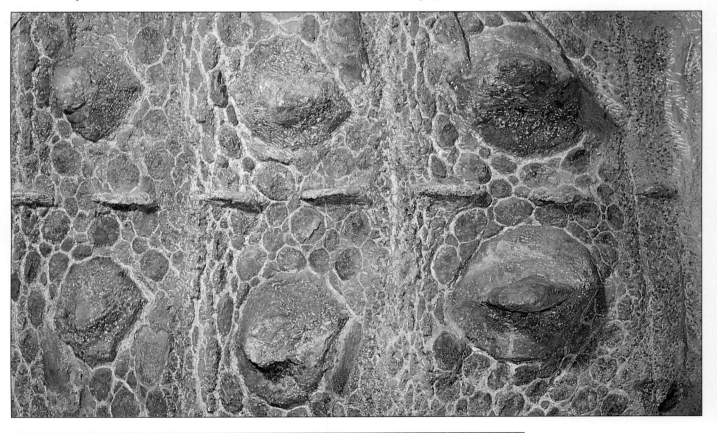

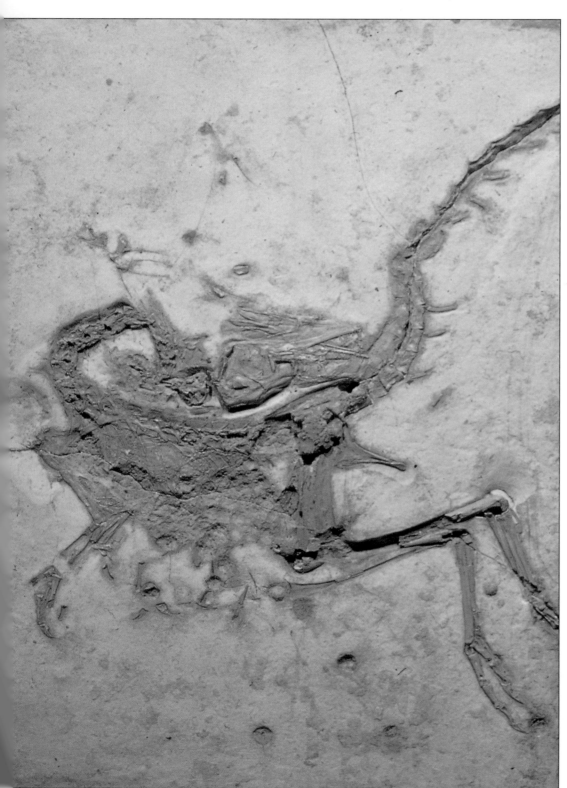

Stomach stones and gut contents

The oddest dinosaurian fossils are stomach contents and stomach stones. Gut contents, like coprolites, give unequivocal information on diet. For example, the tiny Late Jurassic dinosaur *Compsognathus* has been found with the complete, curled-up skeleton of a lizard within its rib cage. The lizard can be identified as *Bavarisaurus*, and we must assume that this creature had been swallowed just before the little dinosaur itself met its fate.

Plant debris is often found scattered around the skeletons of plant-eating dinosaurs. The debris may represent gut contents, but this is usually hard to prove since the material is often similar to other plant remains preserved in the surrounding sediments.

Peculiar rounded, polished stones are also found in association with the rib cages of herbivorous dinosaurs. It is thought the dinosaurs used these stones, termed gastroliths or "stomach stones", in the same way that birds use grit, to grind up food in a gizzard-like section of the gut. Chickens peck for grit, which they store in the gizzard, a muscular bag between mouth and stomach, where grains and other hard foods are ground up before digestion. The bird gizzard is equivalent to our molar (cheek) teeth. Dinosaurs had teeth, but they could not chew since their jaws simply opened and shut like hinges, with no sideways grinding movements. So they may well have had gizzards and gastroliths, but it is hard to demonstrate that all polished pebbles found associated with dinosaur skeletons are indeed true stomach stones, and not chance associations.

Direct evidence of diet. This fossil of the tiny Late Jurassic dinosaur Compsognathus *(left) shows exquisite preservation of all the bones — and, within its rib cage, the complete skeleton of the lizard* Bavarisaurus, *its last meal (highlighted in red above).*

THE WORLD OF THE DINOSAURS

Dinosaurs have been found in all parts of the world, from the famous deposits of North America, exploited since 1850 by dozens of collectors, the classic quarries and coasts of parts of Europe, to more recent finds in China, Australia, and South America. Until 1850, dinosaurs were known from southern England as a result of the studies of men such as Gideon Mantell and William Buckland, from Germany, collected by Hermann von Meyer, and from Montana, USA, collected by Ferdinand Hayden. The collections by these scientists have produced a list of no more than a dozen dinosaur species.

In North America, large specimens were collected in the eastern States, as well as the more prolific midwest, for Joseph Leidy. His important work was soon overshadowed by the fierce rivalry and superhuman collecting endeavours on behalf of Othniel Marsh and Edward Cope. Hundreds of tonnes of dinosaur bones were excavated from Utah, Colorado, Montana, Wyoming, Texas, and surrounding states, revealing dozens of new localities and many new dinosaur names. In Europe, at the same time, many new dinosaurs were recorded from England, France, Belgium, Germany, Hungary, and elsewhere by a large number of palaeontologists. By 1900, as a result, the global total of dinosaurian species must have risen to 200 or more.

Occasional discoveries were also made farther afield, in developing colonial lands in Africa, Australasia, and Asia. However, it was only in this century that serious large-scale excavations were carried out in South Africa, Tanzania, North Africa, India, China, Australia, and South America.

Continental drift — the movement of parts of the Earth's crust relative to each other — is an accepted fact of geology. In the days of the dinosaurs, the continents were nearly all fused together as one great land mass, Pangaea (1). This progressively broke up, first by the opening of the Atlantic Ocean west of northern Africa (2), while the eastern end of Africa and India moved towards Asia (3). The southern Atlantic then opened between South America and Africa (4), and the northern Atlantic appeared a little later (5).

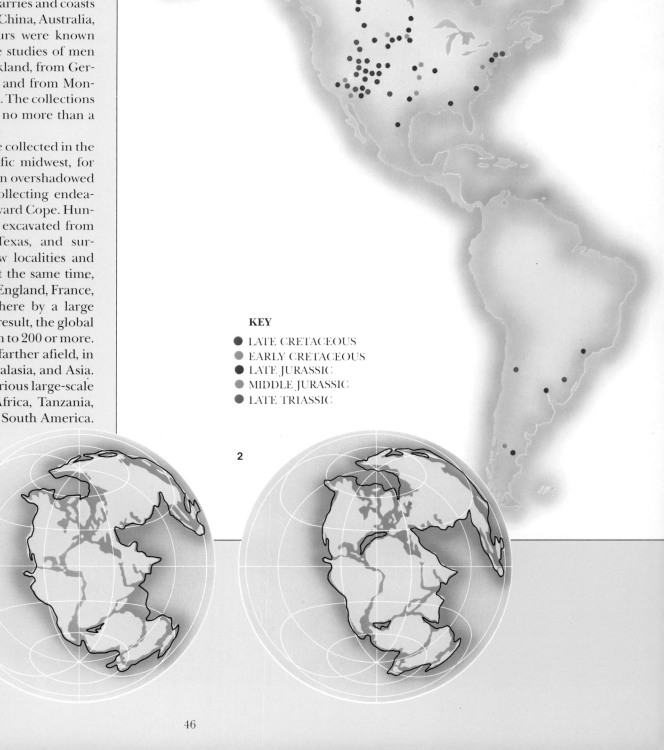

1

2

KEY

● LATE CRETACEOUS
● EARLY CRETACEOUS
● LATE JURASSIC
● MIDDLE JURASSIC
● LATE TRIASSIC

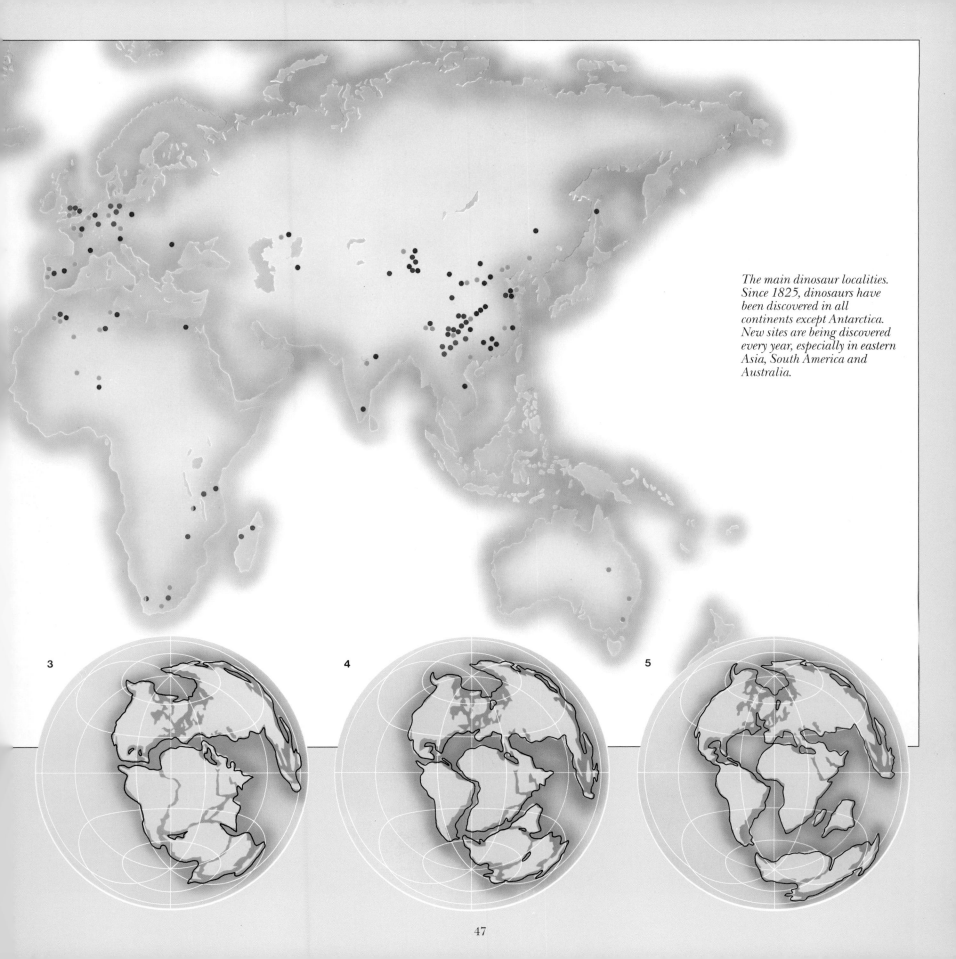

The main dinosaur localities. Since 1825, dinosaurs have been discovered in all continents except Antarctica. New sites are being discovered every year, especially in eastern Asia, South America and Australia.

3

4

5

Collecting dinosaurs

Dinosaur fossils have been collected systematically since about 1830, and the basic techniques have not changed that much. The principle is to extract the skeletons as efficiently as possible, with as little damage as possible. Because most "dinosaur country" is so remote today, and due to the vast bulk of many specimens, the logistics of staffing, maintenance and transport are just as important as the scientific aspects such as interpreting the local environment and the rocks, recording and logging the discoveries precisely, and recovering every last fragment of each specimen.

Dinosaurs have been collected from every continent except Antarctica until recently. However in early 1989 that gap was filled when a dinosaur skeleton was found by geologists and palaeontologists working for the British Antarctic Survey. As has been noted, dinosaurs are found only in rocks dating from the Late Triassic to the end of the Cretaceous (230 to 66 million years old). In addition, they occur commonly only in terrestrial deposits — that is, mudstones and sandstones deposited in rivers or lakes. Rare dinosaur specimens are known from marine sediments, but such finds depend on the remote chance of a carcass being washed down a river and then out to sea.

Ease of discovery is greatest where the appropriate rocks are exposed over large areas and subject to relatively rapid erosion. Hence, some of the richest dinosaur beds today are in the dry, badland-like country of the midwest of North America (Alberta, Montana, Utah, Colorado, Arizona); the open pampas of Argentina and Brazil in South America; the dry savanna of Tanzania, Zimbabwe, South Africa, Niger and Morocco in Africa; the central plains of India; the Gobi Desert in Mongolia; the central and northern plains of China; and the eastern grasslands of Australia. In the past, dinosaur fossils were found in hundreds of localities throughout Europe, but very few are discovered now, because times and fashions have changed. Until about 1900, stone was quarried throughout Europe for building purposes and dozens of dinosaur skeletons were collected by the quarrymen. Now that very little stone is extracted — and where it is, massive machinery does the work — dinosaur skeletons are rare finds.

Naturalists of former centuries took a keen interest in fossils. They were seen as fascinating curiosities, as evidence of life from bygone eras — but they were poorly understood. William Buckland (1784-1856), the discoverer of the first-named dinosaur Megalosaurus, *was also famed for his studies of glaciers, and he is dressed suitably for these researches (above). Bones of large animals were frequently found in caves, as in this example from Holland (right).*

Dinosaur digging can be hard work. A great deal of rock has to be removed in order to expose the bones (left). When the sandstone is well cemented and hard, mechanical equipment such as pneumatic drills, or even explosives may be necessary. The exposed bones are protected from the broken rock by plastic sheets.

The expedition

Most dinosaur-collecting expeditions have to be planned well in advance, maybe years ahead of time, because of the need to obtain funding and recruit the volunteers who do much of the work. Even a basic expedition requires significant sums of money in order to cover the costs of food, communications, tools, transport and wages. The aims are usually to obtain fossils that can be used for both display and research purposes. Research-quality specimens might be whole skeletons or even odd bones if they come from a rare type of dinosaur, whereas display specimens have to be as complete as possible, even if they are quite common animals and already well known to science. There is a growing worldwide demand for display specimens, and museums and educational institutions may be persuaded to fund an expedition since there is a guaranteed "pay-off" in terms of increased numbers of museum visitors or enhanced educational benefits. The best dinosaur discoveries are spectacular display specimens that are also new to science, but these are exceptionally rare! Most dinosaur specimens that excite the expert probably look rather unimpressive to the average museum-goer.

The tibia (shin bone) of a hadrosaur (right), a common find in the Late Cretaceous sediments of Montana. This huge bone has been exposed in the rock after several days of careful work.

A dinosaur bone bed in southern Alberta (above). Bones of a wide range of dinosaurs — hadrosaurs, ceratopsians, ankylosaurs and rare theropods — were jumbled together in a broad deposit, now laid bare by erosion.

Dinosaur bones in the rock may be large, but they are also delicate (right). Dilute adhesives are applied to these hadrosaur hip bones in order to harden them and to stick fractured pieces together.

A dinosaur dig in progress (right). Several palaeontologists work systematically over the surface, removing the rock layer by layer, and exposing the multitudes of bones from several hadrosaurs.

The planning of a dinosaur-collecting expedition is crucial. The area of search must be well defined, and there has to be strong information that skeletons are there — and can be found. This information comes from prospecting. A geologist or palaeontologist tramps along the bottoms of ravines or slopes, in sedimentary rocks of the right age, looking for bone fragments. He or she follows their tracks back up the gullies and ravines until he identifies their source, which may be an unidentifiable lump of weathered bone or a near-complete skeleton. The prospector then attempts to assess what the specimen might be, and how extensive it is, from the exposed pieces of bone. He or she can then report back on whether it is worth spending a few hundred hours excavating the site.

Planning the expedition also involves negotiations with the land owners to clear access to the site and establish the legal right to excavate and remove specimens. Nowadays, this often involves the purchase of a lease or the payment of royalties on any specimens removed. Many classic dinosaur lands are held by the government as natural parks, and collecting is restricted to relevant museums and scientific institutions in order to prevent overworking or excessive commercial exploitation.

The expedition leaders must arrange adequate vehicles that can travel over rough terrain, and carry bones weighing several tonnes! They organize trailers or tents for the crew, safe supplies of water, adequate food, and other day-to-day necessities. These domestic arrangements are crucial since many dinosaur "digs" are hundreds of kilometres from the shops or sanitary facilities, and the crew may have to operate for months in total isolation.

Finally, the leaders arrange for the necessary equipment: hammers, picks, spades, chisels, brushes, sackcloth, plaster and wood. Modern expeditions often take air compressors to operate pneumatic drills, explosives (rarely), casting media (if they hope to take impressions of footprints), surveying equipment, cameras (still and video), short-wave radios, field telephones and other gadgetry.

A well-planned excavation can take as little as a week or as long as a month, depending on how much rock lies above the specimen and the size and extent to which the bones are scattered beneath the surface. When the collectors have guessed the layout of the skeleton, the "overburden" (overlying rock) has to be removed. There may be many tonnes of hard rock to be dug or broken away, and pneumatic drills may be useful here if a compressor can be brought to the site. The aim is to reach a level a few centimetres above the bones as fast as possible, but the amount

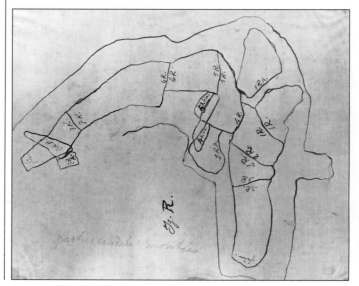

Particularly hard rock is removed with a power drill by a worker at Dinosaur National Monument, Colorado (left). The two limb bones of Allosaurus, *a large theropod, are being prepared for removal by careful channelling around their sides.*

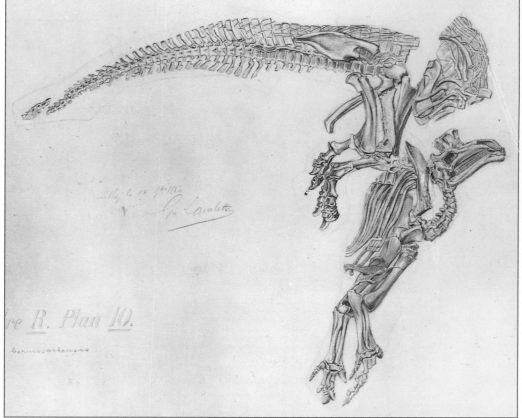

of overburden increases with the steepness of the slope and the scattered extent of the bones to be excavated.

Controlled exposure of the whole skeleton is then carried out by the careful removal of rock from the rough platform, down to the bones themselves. Small pneumatic drills, hammers and chisels, and small pick hammers may be used for this stage of the operation. Once bones are encountered, finer tools such as handle-mounted needles and very light chisels are more appropriate, since the slightest mishit may destroy the delicate bone surface. The bones of a single dinosaur skeleton generally all lie at a single level, which helps the process of excavation considerably. Each bone is traced and "followed out" carefully until it is completely exposed from above. The excavators range outwards in search of more bones, but they can usually predict what they expect to find, and where, if the skeleton is still partially articulated (joined together). In other words, once they have found a single vertebra (backbone) from the neck or tail, they can expect to find more on

Once the site is partially excavated, maps are constructed. The area is criss-crossed by a grid of strings set in one-metre squares. A frame divided into ten-centimetre squares is moved across so that the exact locations of each bone may be precisely recorded (right).

The outline sketch (left) shows how a skeleton of Iguanodon *was divided into 15 plastered blocks in the field when it was excavated in Belgium in 1878. After preparation at the Brussels Museum, the complete skeleton was drawn (below left) exactly as it was preserved.*

either side stretching out in a regular way.

The next stage is crucial: the mapping and recording of the skeleton's layout. If the bones cover a large area, standard surveying equipment is used to measure out a baseline for mapping. Strings may be stretched across the whole site to divide it into metre squares, and the contents of each square are then mapped precisely using a metre square bearing finer grid lines on a transparent sheet. Numerous photographs of the site are taken as back-ups for the map. The map is an essential part of the excavation exercise since it records permanently how the skeleton was preserved in the rock, which may give useful information on "taphonomy": how the animal died, how its skeleton was scavenged, transported, broken up, and finally buried. The photographs and the map are also of critical importance to allow the palaeontologists to reassemble the bones in the laboratory, since it is impossible to remember the exact positions of the dozens of vertebrae, ribs and limb bones of a typical dinosaur skeleton.

The map depicting the layout of the bones may be very detailed, and it serves to show the laboratory technicians how the blocks were arranged in the field. This map of a slab with theropod remains is being supplemented with detailed information on the bones, so that it can be used in studies of their mode of preservation (right).

Preparing the bones for removal. A hadrosaur limb bone is cleared of rock as far as possible, and water is used to loosen the hardened clay (top left). Channels are dug around the bone (left) and it is then covered with damp paper for protection (top right).

Preparing for transport

The bones are then prepared for transport — a hazardous part of the whole exercise. Despite their great size, dinosaur bones can be fragile, and they have to be protected from fracture while they are being lifted and during transit. First, deep trenches are dug around the bones. Isolated bones can be taken out one by one, but masses of overlapping bones have to be removed in single large blocks. The bones are covered with wet paper as a separator, and then strips of sacking (burlap) soaked in plaster are stretched across. Several layers of these "bandages" are applied until the bones are covered with a hard shell, like the plaster cast applied to a broken leg in hospital.

Once the cast has set over the fossil, it is broken free from the underlying rock with crowbars and flipped over. The loose sandstone and shale beneath the bones is picked out, and a plaster cast is applied to the underside of the bones too. It is now enclosed in a tough cocoon and can be moved from the site. Small bones are carried by hand, but larger blocks must be dragged out on sledges or carts. Single major blocks of even a modest-sized dinosaur may weigh five tonnes, and their removal to the waiting vehicles can be a major engineering challenge — especially if the site is a remote and inaccessible ravine.

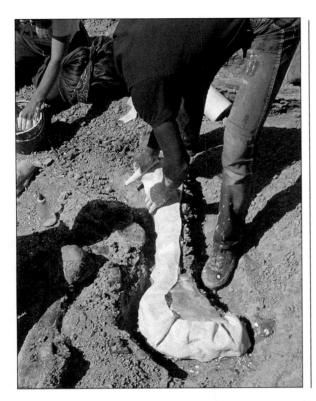

Protecting the bones. Strips of sacking (burlap) soaked in plaster are wrapped around the bone, layer by layer (above), until it is entirely encased over the top and sides (right).

Further plaster is daubed over the top surface (top) and, when it has set, the bone is tipped over ready for final plastering (above).

Clearing and removing large blocks. A block containing the rib cage of a hadrosaur is tipped up after plastering, and the back is cleaned out (above) for final plastering. Large blocks such as these may weigh several tonnes and require a heavy-duty block and tackle to turn them over (right).

Heavy blocks also present problems of transport: how to get them out of the remote and craggy "badland" terrain where the fossils are often found. A crew in Montana uses a homemade wheeled trolley (above).

Transporting dinosaur fossils

The plaster-encased specimens are next carried back to a museum or university for study. Transport can be a major logistical problem for a dinosaur expedition, because of the great weight and bulk of many specimens, because of the rough terrain they often have to be carried over, and because of the sheer distances involved in certain cases.

In the heroic days of dinosaur collecting in North America, during the last century, the bones were carried out of the sites on the backs of horses or in great waggons. They then had to be hauled for many kilometres over the rough "badland" terrain, often without the benefit of roads or tracks, to a railway halt where they could be loaded on goods trains for the long journey east to New York, Washington or a similar centre of learning of the day. The whole journey from the site to the lab could take weeks, and the dangers included appalling weather conditions (the "bone crews" worked all winter in many cases) and hostile Indians, as well as the wear and tear of transport, and mishandling of specimens by unwitting railway porters. Until the last years of the 19th century, dinosaur bones were usually just packed in crates with straw or sacking, and they could suffer a great deal of damage during the journey. The var-

After a long haul, a large block is loaded onto a truck on level ground (top left) for transport to the museum. A heavy block is lowered on chains from the near-vertical bone-bearing face at Dinosaur National Monument (top right).

ious plastering techniques were developed in the late 1870s. One method involved strips of cloth dipped in flour paste, while another was simply to dollop plaster on the outside of the bones. The modern technique described above, in which strips of sacking dipped in plaster are laid over the bones, became standard practice from the 1880s.

At that time, too, palaeontologists themselves often had little field experience. They waited back at the laboratory for the consignments of bones to arrive, with little idea of the context in which they had been collected. This could lead to appalling confusion when they tried to reassemble skeletons: bits and pieces from several different specimens might be incorporated into a single reconstruction, because few records were made of the exact arrangement of the bones in the rock.

Transport now is generally by truck. There are still the dangers of rough terrain around many localities, and bones may still suffer damage even though they are always encased in plaster. However, members of the crew generally accompany the bones, and they have detailed maps of the arrangement of the fossils before these were dug up, as well as photographs. The job of assembly is now rather easier than in the past.

DINOSAURS OF THE MIDDLE JURASSIC

Until recently, Middle Jurassic dinosaurs have been known only from odd finds made in England, France and India. However, major discoveries in China in the past few years have filled a gap.

Although China was remote from the dinosaur beds of Europe, the dinosaurs were rather similar, since continuous land existed between the two areas and climates were warm in most of the world. There were no polar ice caps, and mountain ranges such as the Alps, the Urals, the Himalayas and the Rockies did not exist. Hence, there were few barriers to global migrations by the dinosaurs.

The main groups of dinosaurs represented in the Chinese Middle Jurassic scene are the herbivorous sauropods, a stegosaur and an ornithopod, as well as the carnivorous megalosaur *Gasosaurus*. The larger trees are conifers, and lower plants are ferns and cycads.

How the world looked
in this period

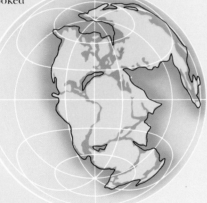

The stegosaur Tuojiangosaurus *(1) was smaller than many of its later relatives, and smaller than the sauropods* Shunosaurus *(2) and* Datousaurus *(3), which were nine metres and 14 metres long respectively. The tiny fabrosaur ornithopod* Xiaosaurus *(4) was ready prey for the megalosaur* Gasosaurus *(5), which was considerably larger than a human being.*

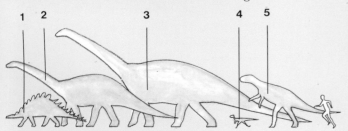

CHAPTER THREE

DINOSAURS IN THE LABORATORY

Excavating a dinosaur skeleton over a period of several weeks, and preparing it carefully for transport, is only the start of the work. The next stages, in the laboratory, may take years and involve different experts with special skills: preparators, who clean up the bones and remove them fully from the remaining "matrix" (the rock around them); conservators, who apply mechanical and chemical treatments to problematical specimens that might otherwise disintegrate; palaeontologists, who study the bones and attempt to interpret what they are and what they tell us; engineers, who prepare the complex frameworks required to mount the skeleton in a natural pose; scientific artists, who draw the bones for publication with the technical description; and designers and educationalists, who present the information to the public in the form of museum displays, books and films.

Preparation of the bones

Dinosaur bone laboratories have to be large to be useful. The best ones are like huge warehouses, with rows of tables in the unloading bay and great racks of industrial-strength steel shelving. The specimens are unloaded and laid out in associated sets so that the laboratory staff can work on one animal, or one closely associated set of bones, at a time.

The first job is to remove the plaster casing. This is done by snipping or slicing through the layers of sackcloth in plaster, but the task has to be done with some care in order

Bones of the Triassic prosauropod Plateosaurus *stored securely in the Stuttgart Museum, West Germany (above). These large limb bones have been cleaned and repaired (note the white plaster) and are kept for study at any time by visiting scientists. The main problems of storage are damp and dust, which can cause these ancient bones to decay.*

The bone lab at the Tyrrell Museum of Palaeontology in Drumheller, Alberta (right). Massive tables support several blocks that have been cut out of their plaster jackets ready for careful exposure.

to minimize the risk of damage. A miniature rotating saw on a flexible drive shaft is ideal for this job. Usually the lower part of the plaster case is left in place beneath a large block, since this provides stability while the technicians work on the bones from above.

Most of the rock matrix has been removed in the field, but the job can be done more precisely and cleanly indoors. If the matrix is soft, it can be picked and scraped off with hand-held chisels and knives. If it is harder, a dental drill is used. This can be held in the hand like a pen, allowing precise movements; the vibrating point is directed in a sweeping motion parallel to or away from the bones, to prevent the risk of slipping and gouging the surface. Typically, this produces a great deal of dust as the rock is scraped away, and a large hood and vacuum tube may be set up over the specimen to keep it clear of debris.

This kind of mechanical preparation is the standard way by which nearly every dinosaur fossil seen in museums has been exposed. It may take days of laborious work to clean up a single bone, but the work is fascinating, almost like sculpting, as the form of the bone progressively makes itself apparent. Fortunately, dinosaur bones are usually hard, smooth on the outside and deep brown in colour, which makes them stand out clearly from the surrounding rock, however hard that is. In 99 per cent of cases, the preparator has no problem distinguishing bone from rock and removing the former from the latter.

There are problem cases, however. For example, the skeleton of the carnivorous dinosaur *Baryonyx*, discovered recently in southern England (see page 80), was partially enclosed in an ironstone nodule. The clay and sandstone

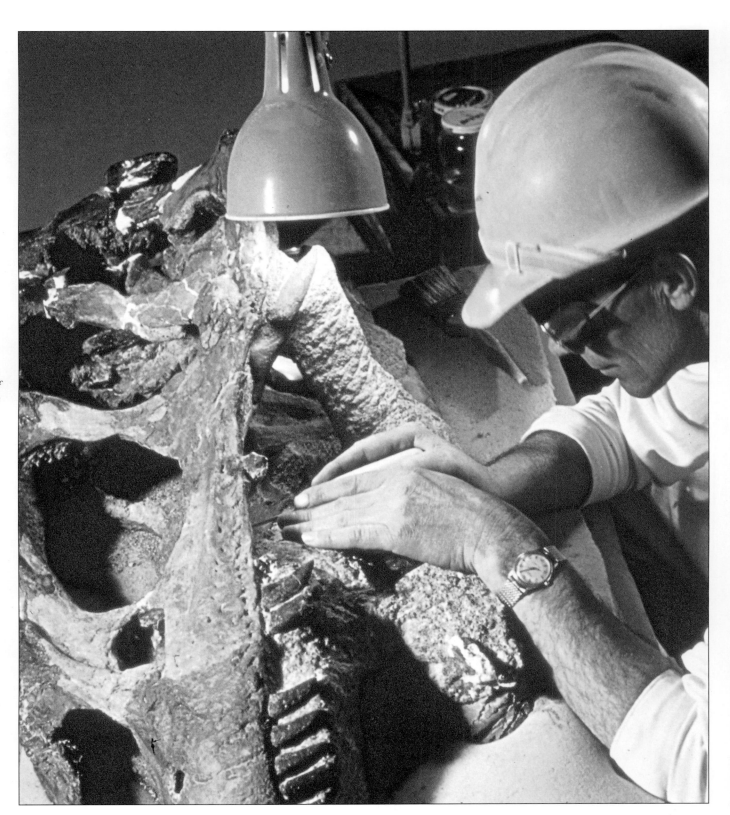

The final stages of preparing a dinosaur may involve weeks of painstaking work with needles and brushes, as the last remnants of the rocky matrix are removed. This excellent skull of Allosaurus *has been exposed in three dimensions and repaired with plaster, ready for exhibition (right).*

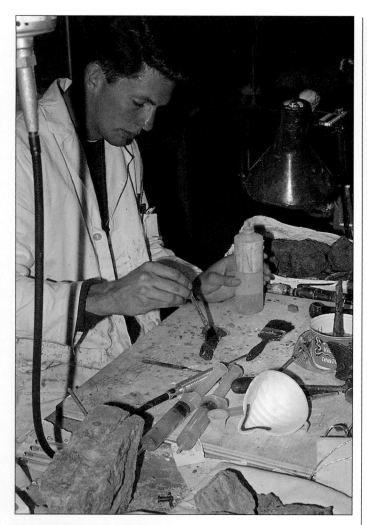

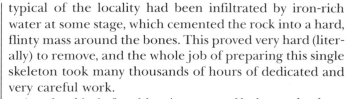

Careful work with a glue brush (left) and small hand drill (above) is necessary to make this fragment of backbone ready for study or exhibition.

Often, a bone is so broken that cracks have to be restored with plaster (left). Gaps in a rib fragment are filled and smoothed flat.

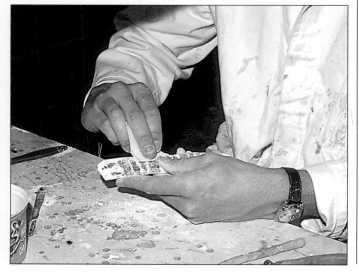

typical of the locality had been infiltrated by iron-rich water at some stage, which cemented the rock into a hard, flinty mass around the bones. This proved very hard (literally) to remove, and the whole job of preparing this single skeleton took many thousands of hours of dedicated and very careful work.

Another kind of problem is presented by bones that have fractured. In some cases the bones are hard enough, but the whole deposit is shot through with tiny fissures, perhaps caused by stresses set up in the Earth's crust at some time in the past. If you attempt to remove the bone from the rock, it falls into thousands of splinters. In such cases, the preparator has to stabilize the bone in its matrix by the use of glues. These are painted over the surface, or introduced into the whole specimen under vacuum. Once the fissures have been filled with glue, the specimen can be cleaned up in the normal way. In other cases of fracture the bone may be friable, possibly as a result of compression or demineralization at some stage after burial. These also have to be stabilized by chemical means, but it may prove impossible to extract a fossil in three dimensions. It may have to be left lying, half-buried, in the rock which acts as a stabilizing support. Of course, such bones cannot be studied — or admired — from all sides.

In nearly all cases, even with the well-preserved, unfissured, and uncompressed examples, some chemical treatment of dinosaur bones is carried out. A thin coating of a

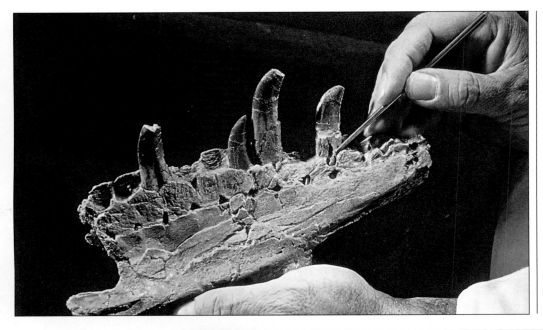

dilute glue or lacquer is applied over the outer surface, simply to provide a tough outer coating. As a result of this the bones can withstand mundane sources of damage such as handling and dusting. A dinosaur skeleton on display may look dark and shiny, like a sleek sports car in a showroom — and this effect is achieved in much the same way in both cases!

When bones are preserved in limestone, the best means of preparation is by acid. Dilute acid slowly breaks down the matrix and exposes the bones without risk of mechanical damage. Usually, dilute acetic acid (the basis of vinegar) is employed since it is less likely to dissolve the bone surface than hydrochloric acid. This acid-etching technique is especially valuable when bones are small and delicate. The specimen to be etched is upended in a shallow bath of acid, diluted to five per cent or less with water, and left for a day or so. It is then removed for examination and washing. If the bones are very delicate, the surface of the slab may be neutralized to remove all traces of the acid, then dried, and

Dinosaur bones ready for study. The last pieces of rock are removed from a perfectly preserved jaw of Allosaurus *(above). New teeth were continuously produced within the jaw bone, and they are covered on the inside by porous bony plates. A near-perfect hadrosaur skull in the museum store after preparation (right). This specimen is mounted and ready for show.*

the bones painted with a thin protective coating of glue. The specimen is completely immersed in a fresh bath of dilute acid and the whole process is repeated, until the bones are laid as bare as possible.

As the preparators clean around the bones, stabilizing them if necessary, they lay the specimens on a bench for regular study. Each bone is logged and compared with field sketches, maps and photographs so that its identity is known. Complex parts of the skeleton, such as the skull, may be pieced together at this stage, if they had become broken or otherwise damaged during fossilization. When all the elements of the assemblage are available, the palae-ontologists, artists and photographers move in.

Making casts

When dinosaur bones turn out to be particularly inter-esting — a new form of dinosaur, perhaps, or a particularly well-preserved one — the palaeontologists may decide to make some casts. The idea is to make replicas of the bones

Drawing the fossil bones is a task that requires a rare mix of scientific and artistic ability (right). The artist in the Tyrrell Museum of Palaeontology, Drumheller, produces an accurate drawing of great scientific value. This will illustrate a monograph describing the dinosaur specimens. Hundreds of such drawings may be made of all the bones of a single dinosaur species, as a guide to restoring its overall appearance.

The author with a hadrosaur skull which he found in the Late Cretaceous sediments of southern Alberta. It is now stored in the Tyrrell Museum, ready for scientific description (above).

A tooth of Megalosaurus *(right) from Sarsden, Oxfordshire. Such a specimen may require relatively little preparatory work before it is ready for study.*

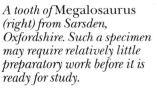

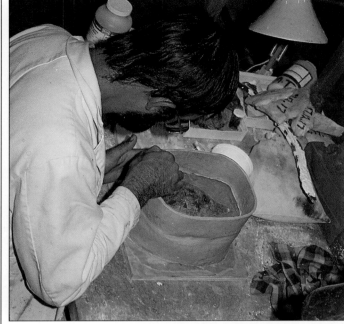

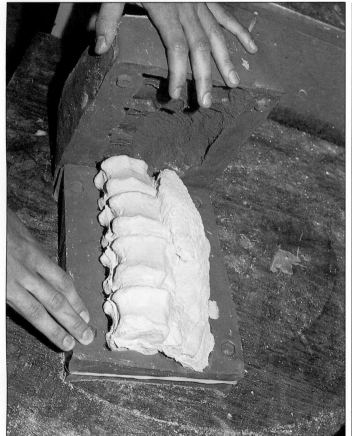

Making casts: two hadrosaur skulls, including a crested form in a half mould (top left). The first task in making a cast is to produce a mould from the original specimen (top right). The mould is formed from flexible plastic or rubber, which is poured into a well built around the specimen. The mould is made in two or more pieces.

Dozens of casts can be made from the moulds. This cast of tail bones was produced by pouring plaster or a plastic material into the moulds. After setting, the flexible moulds are peeled apart, revealing a perfect cast (left).

that are as accurate and realistic as possible. The first task is to produce moulds from the original bones. This must be done carefully in order to avoid damage to the specimens. Nowadays, moulds are usually made from flexible, rubbery plastics which can be peeled off the bone, and then the cast, with ease. Formerly the whole procedure was done with ordinary plaster, but the results could be crude.

The main problem in making a mould of a bone is, perhaps surprisingly, designing the shape of the mould. A mould always consists of two or more pieces which must hold together precisely while the cast is being poured, so that there is no distortion, but which must then pull apart cleanly. The design of moulds is fairly straightforward for typical limb bones or vertebrae, since they can be made in two matching halves, with small knobs and sockets along the join line to hold them together firmly during pouring. When the specimen is a complex three-dimensional shape, like a skull or a hip girdle, much more care is required. The mould may be made from a dozen or more separate units, all of which must fit together accurately, and then pull apart in a controlled sequence once the cast has had a chance to harden inside.

Casts of bones are usually made with some hard plastic or plaster compound. Large bones may even be cast in glass fibre. The benefits over the old-fashioned plain plaster of Paris are several: the cast is much tougher, and can withstand rough treatment; it is often lighter and easier to

A more complex cast (left) sees the light. The two pieces of the flexible mould (red latex) key together tightly so that the casting material does not leak out.

Half of the mould has been removed (above), revealing the dome-shaped top of a pachycephalosaur (bone-head) skull.

Two casts (below) show the final result, after careful colouring of the plaster to match the original bone. One value of having casts is that they can be cut in half!

handle; and it can be coloured and treated before setting to reproduce the look of real bones. In the old days, artists had to paint the outside surface of a plaster cast to mimic fossil bone colours, but they could not imitate the sheen, and any cracks or knocks left white marks. Most of the mounted dinosaur skeletons seen in museums today are high-quality casts, and newer ones are very hard to distinguish from the real thing except on detailed examination.

Many casts may be made from one mould. It is common for large dinosaur museums to maintain stocks of casts of their best specimens, for multiple mounts and exchange. A single original skeleton may give rise to dozens of nearly identical replicas in this way. Sets of bones can then be exchanged with other museums, who require a particular specimen for display or study. It is also possible to make effective displays consisting of a number of skeletons of one species of dinosaur, arranged in various poses — and all made from casts of the same original skeleton.

Pachycephalosaur Brain Case

From the outside, the dome-headed pachycephalosaurs may have looked quite intelligent. Surely such large skulls housed well-developed brains. This was not the case. In the cross section you can see the actual size of the brain.

DINOSAUR DEVELOPMENT

The Theropoda, all carnivores, lived for the entire 160 million years of the existence of the dinosaurs. They all fed on other dinosaurs and various smaller animals, and their skeletons show a common structure despite their long evolutionary span and great range in size. All theropods were bipeds (two-legged) and, unlike the herbivorous groups, never used their forelimbs in walking. Indeed, the forelimbs progressively lost nearly all function, becoming much reduced in size during the evolution of the group. The hindlimbs were adapted for rapid locomotion, being strongly built, long and provided with powerful muscles. The limbs were placed directly beneath the body, as seen in a front view of *Tyrannosaurus*, which is most efficient for rapid running.

The theropods varied considerably in size. Some, such as Coelophysis *(2), were on a human scale (1), while the giant* Tyrannosaurus *(3) was the largest carnivorous animal ever on land. The* ornithomimid Struthiomimus *(4) was larger than* Compsognathus *(5), possibly the smallest of all dinosaurs, and* Deinonychus *(6), an agile, human-sized hunter.*

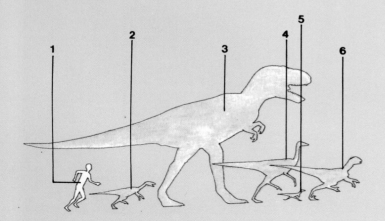

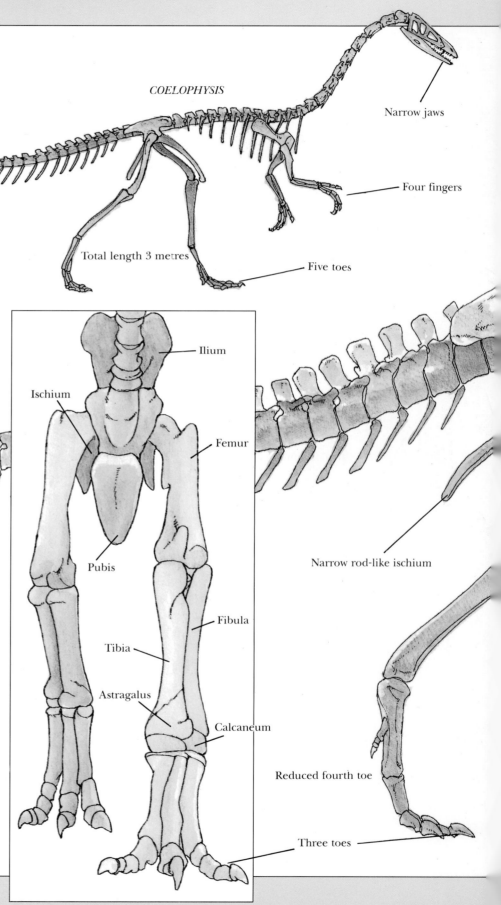

COELOPHYSIS

Narrow jaws

Four fingers

Total length 3 metres

Five toes

Ilium

Ischium

Femur

Pubis

Fibula

Tibia

Astragalus

Calcaneum

Narrow rod-like ischium

Reduced fourth toe

Three toes

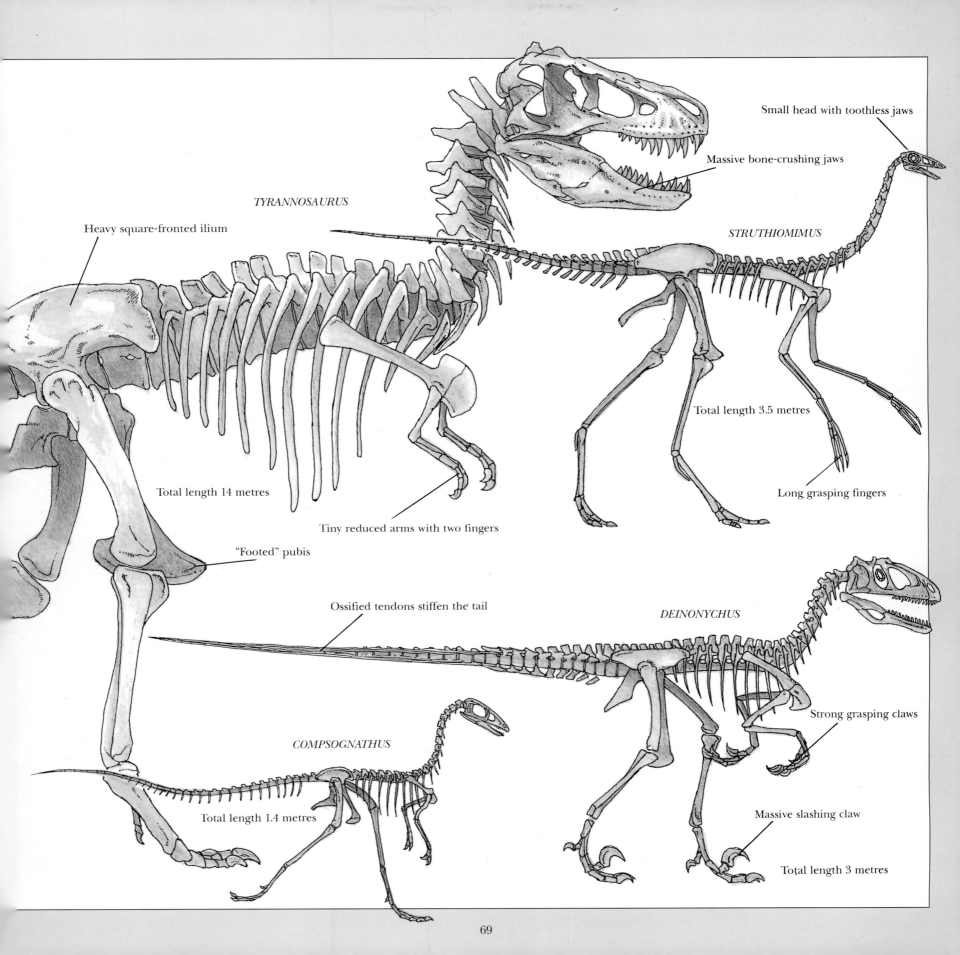

TYRANNOSAURUS

Small head with toothless jaws

Heavy square-fronted ilium

Massive bone-crushing jaws

STRUTHIOMIMUS

Total length 3.5 metres

Total length 14 metres

Long grasping fingers

Tiny reduced arms with two fingers

"Footed" pubis

Ossified tendons stiffen the tail

DEINONYCHUS

Strong grasping claws

COMPSOGNATHUS

Total length 1.4 metres

Massive slashing claw

Total length 3 metres

Reconstructing the skeleton

Dinosaur skeletons are reconstructed — that is, "mounted" and strung together in the correct arrangement of bones and in a natural pose — for two reasons. The first is for display, the second is for scientific study. A palaeontologist who examines the bones laid out in the field can usually make a shrewd assessment of the nature of the new dinosaur find, how complete it is and which type it represents. Back in the lab when the months of preparation are completed, he or she can check the judgement and decide on the fate of the specimen.

Decisions at this stage are vital. If the specimen is to be displayed, the job of mounting the skeleton and exhibiting it may take weeks of skilled work and involve considerable expense. If the skeleton appears to belong to an entirely new species of dinosaur, or if it shows parts of the skeleton from a known dinosaur but which have not been seen before, it is important that the information is passed to other scientists. This course of action also involves a large commitment of time and money — often more than if the specimen is simply prepared for display. Typically, a well-preserved and fairly complete dinosaur skeleton takes some two or three years of a palaeontologist's time, and a year or so for the scientific artist (often they are one and the same person). A new dinosaur skeleton may simultaneously undergo scientific study and be prepared for display in this fashion.

The majority of bones that pass through a dinosaur lab are shelved immediately. They all have some scientific and educational value, but it is impossible to examine everything right away. The larger dinosaur museums have hundreds or thousands of specimens stored away and ready for use. This may seem a great waste of exciting specimens, but even the most ardent dinosaur-lover does not want to look at dozens of similar bones — only the best ones are put on display. The bone stores can be thought of as archives of information, readily available to any serious scholar who is attempting to solve a scientific problem.

A skeleton of Triceratops *(left) mounted in the British Museum (Natural History) in London. The bones are supported on a metal framework, and they are arranged in as lifelike a posture as possible.*

The huge skeleton of Brachiosaurus *from Tanzania, as mounted in the Humboldt Museum, East Berlin (right). This spectacular skeleton is an example of the best kind of display specimen — nearly complete, and well mounted on a complex gantry of steel rods and strips.*

The major dinosaur museums host dozens of visiting scientists every month. These visitors arrive because there are specific specimens they wish to study, which they have seen listed in the catalogues of the museum's collection. One scientist may be reviewing the teeth of the giant carnivore *Tyrannosaurus*, and he needs to look at hundreds of jaws and teeth of this animal and its relatives, stored in various museums on each continent. Another palaeontologist may be trying to identify an unusual new skeleton she has found in France. She has to visit collections in all parts of the world in order to compare the new bones with similar ones found elsewhere. A third palaeontologist may be trying to understand the dynamics of a particular dinosaur population, and for this purpose he has to make a census of everything that has ever been found in a particular rock formation; such specimens may well be scattered in several different museums.

Dinosaur skeletons are mounted by museum technicians, on frameworks made by engineers, and under the watchful eye of a palaeontologist who directs the operation. The palaeontologist knows which bone is which from experience gained by studying other dinosaur skeletons. Every dinosaur, however big or small, has a comparable femur (thigh bone), scapula (shoulder blade), tail vertebrae (backbone), and so on. With such experience, there is little chance of stringing the bones together wrongly, for example by putting the head on the end of the tail vertebrae instead of the neck vertebrae — although this has hap-

Classic museum mounts of dinosaur skeletons: a large Brontosaurus *(top left) in the East Berlin museum, and the bizarre crested plant-eater,* Ouranosaurus *from North Africa (top right). These specimens inspire awe because of their great size and unusual appearance.*

An unusual head-first shot of the Chinese sauropod Shunosaurus *(right) shows its broad, leaf-like teeth and long neck.*

pened in the past! The palaeontologist also has the field maps and photographs to help place any questionable bones in their correct positions. Problems generally arise only when individual bones are damaged, or where some of the bones are missing.

Once the bones have been laid out in their correct anatomical positions, the engineer designs and constructs an armature, which is the metal framework on which the bones will be mounted. The principles of construction depend on whether the original bones or casts are being used in the mount. A cast is much lighter, and so needs less support, and small screws or rods can be inserted into the different parts with impunity. Indeed, it is possible to make an "invisible mount" for a cast of a dinosaur skeleton, composed entirely of internal rods.

Traditional armatures for holding bones in place are usually made from strips of steel that run beneath each bone. The strips are shaped precisely by heating to high temperatures, and are then supported on vertical pillars. The strips and pillars are made as discreetly as possible, so that they will be largely concealed by bones when the skeleton is eventually mounted for exhibition, but at the same time they must be capable of supporting the great weight of the fossil bones. A newer technique is to support each bone, particularly the vertebrae, on strong transparent strings hanging from the ceiling of the display room. This avoids the need for a complex armature, and the bones can easily be lifted out for individual study.

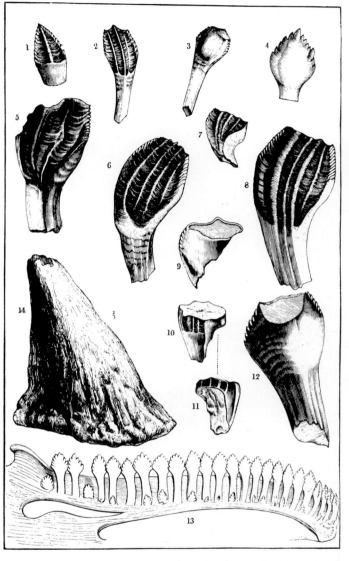

Studying the bones

The palaeontologist studies each bone in turn, to establish its exact structure and relationships with other bones. If the bone is damaged or distorted, attempts are made to restore it to the original shape. This may be done with modelling clay, or imaginatively in two dimensions on paper. Detailed drawings are made of each bone viewed from several angles. The standard views are from above and below (dorsal and ventral views), from the front and the back (anterior and posterior views), and from the sides (lateral views). Such drawings have features of a technical engineering drawing, since they need to be absolutely accurate in outline and in orientation for the standard views. For very large bones, drawings are usually scaled down to a more manageable size.

Some features of the drawings are less technical and tend towards the more artistic and interpretative. Shading is applied to indicate the three-dimensional form of the bone, either by dot shading (the dots are closest together in the deepest parts of the specimen) or narrow-line shading (hatching). In addition, special features such as blood vessel openings and muscle scars on the bones are shown clearly. The whole specimen is labelled carefully to identify every part and feature.

Dinosaurs have always attracted large audiences! Richard Owen (1804-1892) gives a Friday Evening Discourse at the Royal Institution, London, in 1849 (above). An original plate (right) from William Buckland's Geology and Mineralogy *(1836) illustrates a comparison of the fossil teeth and nasal horn from the second dinosaur to be named,* Iguanodon, *with the lower jaw and teeth from the living lizard,* Iguana.

Series of photographs are often taken in the study of dinosaur bones, and they may be used as the basis for drawings since they provide accurate proportions. Photographs of dinosaur bones accompany the scientific descriptions to some extent, but drawings are usually preferred, because a certain amount of interpretation can be put into the drawings. This might sound like a "bad thing", a possible source of imaginary sketches which are not accurate. However, minor surface damage and cracks on the bones can be omitted; the surface shine on a bone may also produce patches of glare in a photograph, which can be omitted in the drawing. Important features can be highlighted to an extent in a drawing too by the use of shading.

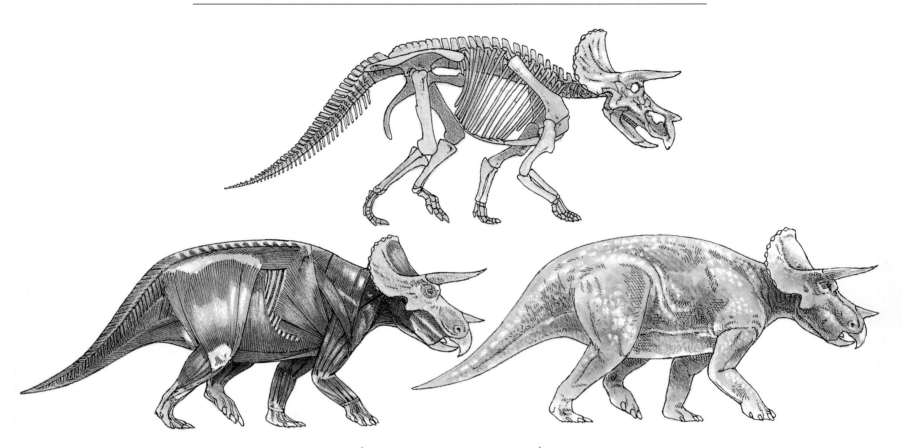

Describing and interpreting

The palaeontologist prepares a formal description of each bone available, and prepares this part of the report in a fairly standardized sequence. Normally the skull is described first, then the vertebral column (spine) from front to back, then the shoulder girdle and arms, the hip girdle and legs, and finally minor surface elements such as the ribs or scales. Within this framework, the skull description is also formalized. The palaeontologist directs attention to the snout first, then moves back over the top of the head, around the sides, inside over the palate, then round the intricacies of the braincase, along the lower jaw, and finally around the teeth. The description of a well-preserved dinosaur skull can easily occupy 50 or more pages of an average scientific report, since there is so much detail. The descriptive portions of the account are keyed in with matching illustrations that show the parts being described.

The report then moves on to more interpretative aspects of the find. These may include chapters to do with jaw mechanics and limb mechanics — in other words, how the animal ate and how it moved about. There are a number of approaches to these questions, which are firmly grounded in knowledge derived from living animals. For example, if the details of the fossil bones are well preserved, the palae-

Reconstructing the life appearance of the ornithopod Triceratops *is a three-stage process. First, the skeleton is restored in detail and posed as naturally as possible (top). Then the muscles are reconstructed using evidence from the bone surfaces and from comparisons with living animals (bottom left). Finally, the skin is placed over the muscles and other soft parts, and it is drawn using evidence from living animals that have similar lifestyles (bottom right).*

ontologist can speculate with some confidence on the nature of the jaw and limb joints. By holding and manipulating the fossil bones, he or she can establish how far they could move with respect to each other, and in which directions. Next, the complex musculature that operated the moving jaw or limb can be reconstructed. The bones bear muscle scars, which are compared to those of modern animals such as crocodiles or birds. This allows informed guesses at the positions of the muscles, their size and directions of action. The expert can have some confidence in these speculations, since all living vertebrates share many common patterns in their muscles by virtue of their shared common ancestry, and there is no reason to suppose that dinosaurs were wildly different!

Finally, the palaeontologist attempts to pull together all this information and work out, for example, the power and direction of jaw movements. Combined with other evidence, such as the shapes of the teeth, their patterns of wear, and associated animals and plants at the site, this assists speculations on diet and feeding. The shapes of the limb bones, the postulated limb muscles, and evidence from fossilized trackways can allow detailed proposals on how the animal walked and ran.

Once the palaeontologist has studied every bone in

detail, and attempted to interpret the moving parts, he or she puts together all of the information in an overview of what the animal looked like and how it lived. A mounted skeleton of the whole animal, detailed drawings of the whole skeleton in natural poses, and reconstructions of the jaw and limb muscles may be available to assist in the task of restoring other soft parts, such as the head muscles, snout, eyes, ear openings, throat skin, major internal organs and so on. This information is sometimes passed to an artist, who uses it to sculpt a three-dimensional scale model of the animal as it looked in life, or to make a lifelike colour illustration. There is a scientific purpose behind these exercises, as well as an educational one (such reconstructions are used in books such as this one, and in museum displays).

The end-point of this aspect of the palaeontologist's work is to find out as much as possible about how the animal lived and what it looked like. This information can then be used in reconstructing the biology of the species and in recreating the environment in which it lived.

Naming a dinosaur

The second interpretative pathway that the palaeontologist follows is to interpret the evolutionary position of the dinosaur. Is it identical to a dinosaur already described, or is it new? If new, it must be christened with a name consisting of two parts: a generic name, for example *Tyrannosaurus* or *Baryonyx*, and a specific name, such as *Tyrannosaurus rex* or *Baryonyx walkeri*. The first means "tyrant reptile king", the second "heavy claw [in honour of] Walker". The names should convey something important about the animal — its size, terrible appearance, or massive claws — and the specific name may tell us who found it. *Baryonyx* was found by the amateur fossil collector William Walker, and the name is an honour and a means for the palaeontological world to express its thanks to the discoverer.

Naming the animal is not that important, of course, although it must have a name of sorts. The precise name is chosen at the whim of the describer, and any words can be used so long as they are new and not offensive. It is more important to try to understand the relationships of the new

TYRANNOSAURUS REX

Tyrannosaurus rex, *probably the best-known dinosaur, was the largest meat-eating land animal of all time.*

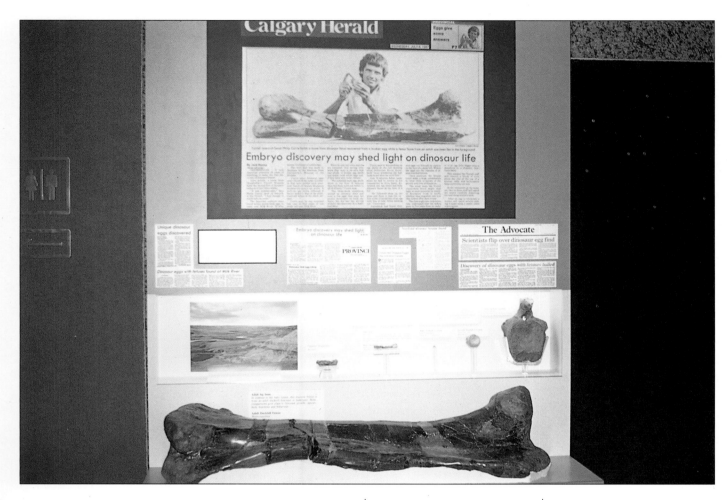

Dinosaurs in the news. Museums display their new finds, like this hadrosaur limb bone (left), and the discoveries are often reported in the press.

dinosaur. What is it related to, and how closely? Is it a new species of a familiar genus, such as *Tyrannosaurus* (which is already well known) or is it a new genus, like *Baryonyx*, which is more distantly related to known forms. Indeed, it has so far proved difficult even to decide to which family *Baryonyx* belongs, whether to the Dromaeosauridae, Ornithomimidae or Spinosauridae. This is like being unable to decide whether a new furry animal from the deepest jungles of Borneo is a dog, cat or bear!

In trying to understand the relationships of a new dinosaur, the palaeontologist wants to see where it fits into the evolutionary scheme. Is it a member of a group that was evolving quickly at the time? Is it the first tyrannosaur, or the first brontosaur, to appear on Earth? Could it perhaps be the last of its group? Large-scale charts of dinosaur evolution, like that on pages 18-19, are built up from hundreds of small interpretations on the evolutionary position of each species.

A cartoon of Gideon Mantell (1790-1852), who discovered fossils of Iguanodon.

Publication

The end of the palaeontologist's job — at least for a while — is to prepare the description, drawings and interpretations of the dinosaur as a manuscript for publication in a scientific journal. This is an essential exercise, for two reasons. Firstly, the work will be scrutinized carefully by two or three other experts in the field, who will assess its quality and suitability for publication. These "scientific referees", as they are called, may make a variety of suggestions for improving the manuscript, ranging from important matters of misinterpretation or omission, to minor changes of spelling and punctuation. The second important reason for publishing the description is simply to put it on record, to make it available to interested scientists elsewhere. Indeed, dinosaur descriptions made over a century ago are still used constantly today, because they summarize information that is needed in modern dinosaur studies — and they usually do it very well.

DINOSAURS OF THE LATE JURASSIC

Some of the best known and most popular dinosaurs lived in the Late Jurassic of North America and Africa. This scene, in Tanzania 150 million years ago, shows a typical group of giant sauropods in the background, a stegosaur, the hypsilophodontid ornithopod *Dryosaurus* (centre right) and an early ornithomimid theropod *Elaphrosaurus* (centre left), a fleet-footed carnivore.

The Late Jurassic scene is dominated by tall conifers and waterside horsetails and cycads. Other typical animals include rat-like mammals, freshwater turtles, crocodiles (not shown), and pigeon-sized pterosaurs with long tails and pointed fish-spearing teeth.

How the world looked in this period

The sauropods from Tanzania include the diplodocids Dicraeosaurus *(1) and* Barosaurus *(2), up to 20 and 27 metres long respectively, and the brachiosaurid* Brachiosaurus *(3), up to 12 metres tall. Other herbivores include the stegosaur* Kentrosaurus *(4) and the hypsilophodontid* Dryosaurus *(5), while the only known carnivorous dinosaur is* Elaphrosaurus *(6), a lightly built, speedy ornithomimid. The last three are all about human-sized.*

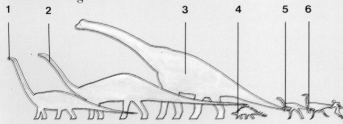

CHAPTER FOUR

DINOSAUR BIOLOGY

The main driving force for most palaeontologists is a desire to find out how animals of the past lived. There are no creatures quite like the dinosaurs on the Earth today, so that exploring their biology is almost like studying life on another planet. At present, palaeontologists in many countries are studying the modes of life of numerous kinds of dinosaurs. Some of their results are presented here.

Baryonyx, the "Super-claw"

One of the most important new dinosaur discoveries of recent years is *Baryonyx*, from the south of England. The first remains were collected early in 1983 by William Walker, a keen amateur fossil collector, from a brick-clay pit in Surrey. He knew that he was likely to find dinosaur bones in this brick pit, since bones of *Iguanodon* and crocodiles had already been discovered there, in rocks of the right age (Lower Cretaceous) and the right sort (sandstones and clays deposited in coastal rivers). The specimen collected by William Walker was a massive claw broken into three or four main pieces. Around its outer curve, the claw measured 31 centimetres. Clearly this was no ordinary claw!

Walker took this spectacular fossil to the British Museum (Natural History) in London, where palaeontologists confirmed its uniqueness. They arranged a full-scale dig at the site, although they did not expect to find much more of the skeleton since the site was being worked by great scraping machines for brick clay. In the end, much of the skeleton

The Chinese theropod Gasosaurus *(opposite), showing its teeth and claws. These provide crucial evidence on the diet and other habits of this early carnivore.*

and skull of "Super-claw", as it had been nicknamed, was recovered. Unfortunately, most of the bones were enclosed in a hard ironstone nodule which has taken several years to remove. In the end, however, the skull and skeleton of "Super-claw" threw up many more surprises when the palaeontologists at last came to study them.

The first scientific report on "Super-claw" was made in 1986, when Drs Angela Milner and Alan Charig of the British Museum (Natural History) published a short description in the international science journal *Nature*. *Baryonyx* turned out to have the body of a theropod dinosaur, akin to *Megalosaurus* or *Tyrannosaurus*, but it had the head of a crocodile. The skull was long and low, and the narrow snout was lined with dozens of small, recurved teeth. This was entirely unexpected, since most theropods had deep jaws armed with relatively small numbers of large teeth — the best set of adaptations for killing prey animals and tearing their flesh. The narrow jaws of *Baryonyx* would have been too weak to grapple with large prey animals, and the teeth unable to cope with tough skin and bone.

What of the massive claw? There was unfortunately no evidence to show whether the claw was from the hand or foot. This may sound ridiculous when a fair amount of the skeleton is known, but the bones have to be found in connection, with the relevant joints well enough preserved to fit them together, for a palaeontologist to be confident. The claw, by analogy with living animals with large claws, was probably used for slashing at prey.

How did *Baryonyx* live? It was a meat-eater, and frequented warm, wet conditions on lowlands covered with rich subtropical vegetation. There were many rivers and

lakes in the area, and these contained a variety of fish. Indeed, some fish scales of a primitive bony fish called *Lepidotes*, an ancient relative of the modern Sturgeon, were found in the region of the rib cage of *Baryonyx*. Milner and Charig suggested that *Baryonyx* fed on fish, which would explain its crocodile-like head. They could not comment on whether it did so in a crocodile-like manner, by swimming powerfully in lakes and rivers, or by snapping into the water from the bank, because the limb bones were not well enough known. Subsequent correspondence in *Nature* included the proposal that *Baryonyx* might have fished in the way that brown bears do in Canada, by scooping prey out of rivers with their great paws. The claw itself may have been a kind of fish scoop. Another correspondent suggested that *Baryonyx* was a vulture-like scavenger, feeding on dinosaur carcasses.

This illustrates the problems, and fascinations, of study-

The great 31-centimetre slashing claw of Baryonyx walkeri *found in Surrey, England, in 1983. This claw may have been used to kill plant-eating dinosaurs.*

COELOPHYSIS

Coelophysis *from the Late Triassic of the United States. Named in 1889, specimens of this theropod have been found in America, Europe, South Africa and South America. It ran on two legs, which freed its hands to catch small prey.*

ing dinosaur biology. Bones can tell palaeontologists a great deal, but they have their limitations. In the case of *Baryonyx* there is some hope, since not all the bones have been prepared in the lab, and they have all yet to undergo full study. Also, more specimens may be found, since the brick pit is still operating, and fossil collectors frequently scour it for new finds turned up by the digging machines.

The small meat-eaters

How typical is *Baryonyx* of other meat-eating dinosaurs? The theropods include a surprising diversity of carnivorous dinosaurs, ranging from the chicken-sized *Compsognathus* from the Late Jurassic of Germany (surely capable of eating nothing larger than a grasshopper or tiny shrew-like mammal) to the monstrous *Tyrannosaurus*, tall as a house and the largest carnivorous animal of all time.

The first theropod dinosaurs were moderate-sized carnivores like *Coelophysis* from the Late Triassic of the United

The lightly-built Ornitholestes *(below) from the Late Jurassic of North America, as mounted in the Tyrrell Museum, Alberta. The long arms with strong fingers were clearly used for manipulating food. The skull is also powerfully built, with a deep lower jaw.*

States. *Coelophysis* was named in 1889 on the basis of several vertebrae, two partial femora (thigh bones) and a sacrum (part of the hip bone) from the Chinle Formation of New Mexico (now dated at about 225 million years old). Further specimens have since been reported from Texas, Connecticut and Arizona, as well as Germany, South Africa and South America, but it is uncertain how much of this material truly belongs to *Coelophysis*. The best collections were made in 1947 and 1948 when a team from the American Museum of Natural History excavated dozens of skeletons from a single site at Ghost Ranch, New Mexico.

This remarkable collection of fossils has yet to be studied in detail, but they show many interesting biological features. *Coelophysis* has a slender skeleton, with a long whip-like tail which was used as a counterbalance when it ran at speed. The creature ran bipedally, which freed its arms for manipulation, and its hands were no doubt efficient in grasping small prey animals and tearing them apart. One

of the skeletons in the Ghost Ranch collection contains the remains of a young *Coelophysis*, which may be an embryo about to be born. However, this skeleton is sufficiently well developed so that it is more likely to be a juvenile that has been eaten. In any case, there is no reason to suppose that *Coelophysis* did not lay eggs like other dinosaurs. So this may be the first recorded case of dinosaur cannibalism!

Other theropods included a range of small to medium-sized, agile forms that fed on non-dinosaur prey and juvenile dinosaurs. Some theropods, oddly, lost their teeth altogether. This would seem inexplicable, since teeth like steak knives were their hallmark. They included the struthiomimids, or "ostrich dinosaurs", which were slender, long-limbed animals that doubtless ran as fast as racehorses. They had powerful arms with long, slender fingers for grasping food, and their toothless jaws must have been covered by a horny beak in life, like the beak of a turtle or bird. This would have been adequate to cut up meat.

An unusual theropod from the Late Cretaceous of Mongolia, *Oviraptor*, shares some of these characters. The first skeleton was found in 1928 lying on top of a nest of *Protoceratops* eggs and the name *Oviraptor* ("egg thief") indicated its presumed diet. Certainly, this dinosaur had deep, oddly-shaped jaws which could have delivered a strong bite to crack any eggshell. Indeed, the bite could have been too strong for that, and it seems likely that *Oviraptor* might well have had another diet.

The dromaeosaurids, such as *Deinonychus* from the Early Cretaceous of Montana, have only been known in detail since the 1960s, although partial specimens were found much earlier. *Deinonychus* was a modest-sized animal, evidently agile and fast-moving, and equipped with its famous slashing claws on the hind feet. Prof. John Ostrom, of the Peabody Museum, Yale University, Connecticut, described the complete anatomy of *Deinonychus* on the basis of new specimens in 1969, and suggested that it may have been a

OVIRAPTOR

Oviraptor was one of the most unusual theropods. Although related to typical meat-eaters such as Tyrannosaurus *and* Coelophysis, *with their long meat-cutting fangs,* Oviraptor *had no teeth at all. Its jaw bones were covered with a horny beak which could probably cut through flesh just as modern birds and turtles can.* Oviraptor *also had powerful, long-fingered hands and it has been suggested that it fed on eggs.*

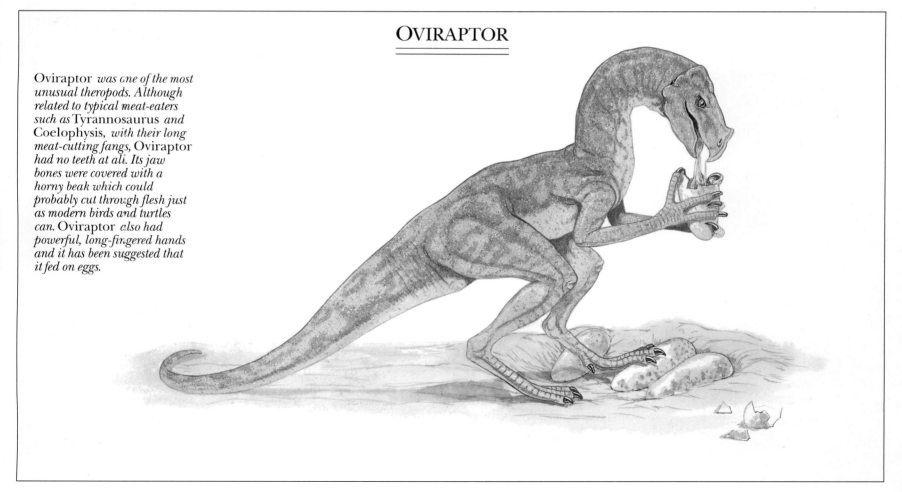

The skull of the biggest meat-eating land animal of all time, Tyrannosaurus rex *from the Late Cretaceous of North America (left). The long knife-like teeth are at the front of the jaw for maximum biting force, and the deep lower jaw indicates very powerful muscles. Notice the extra joint in the middle of the lower jaw which allowed the mouth to open extremely wide.*

pack hunter, like modern wolves and hunting dogs. A group would trail larger herbivorous dinosaurs, snapping at their limbs until they weakened and keeled over.

The tyrannosaurs

Tyrannosaurs lived in the Late Cretaceous, especially in North America and Mongolia, where they preyed on plant-eating hadrosaurs in particular. At 14 metres long, *Tyrannosaurus* was the largest theropod, big enough to tackle almost any herbivorous dinosaur other than the sauropods. The strangest aspect of *Tyrannosaurus* is the contrast between its massive jaws and powerful hindlimbs, and its tiny arms each equipped with only two short fingers. These arms were so short that they did not even reach the mouth, and clearly they could not have been used to grapple with prey or to pass food to the mouth. The function of the arms remained a mystery until 1970, when Barney Newman of London's British Museum (Natural

DEINONYCHUS

Deinonychus, *a spectacular theropod, was discovered in the Early Cretaceous rocks of Montana in the early 1960s.* Deinonychus *is a dromaeosaurid, a group previously known only from partial skeletons from Mongolia and North America.*

The discovery of near-complete skeletons of Deinonychus *allowed Prof. John Ostrom of Yale University to reconstruct the whole body.* Deinonychus *probably hunted in packs, killing large plant-eating dinosaurs with slashing blows from its great foot claw.*

History) suggested that they may have been used to help *Tyrannosaurus* stand up. Large mammals, such as giraffes and elephants, seem to have a slight struggle as they stand up, because the head and neck have to be hoisted clear of the ground at some stage. *Tyrannosaurus* had a massive head and no obvious way of raising it from the ground — other than with its slender arms. Newman postulated that, from a flat-out posture, *Tyrannosaurus* pumped its arms against the ground and threw its head back quickly; at the same time, it lifted the hind quarters on its powerful legs. Thus, the great head swung to its upright position some six metres off the ground in a single, smooth movement. Without the use of its tiny arms, *Tyrannosaurus* might have had even greater trouble in getting up and going, first thing in the morning.

Was *Tyrannosaurus* really a voracious predator, that tore through the Late Cretaceous woodlands slashing and chomping at every dinosaur it encountered? Or did it live a more sedate life, mainly scavenging on dinosaur carcasses? Both views have been proposed recently, and they typify part of the debate about whether dinosaurs were warm-blooded or not (see pages 112-117). It seems likely that *Tyrannosaurus* was so massive it could not have rushed about in a violent manner. Indeed, many of its prey animals were probably fleeter of foot (the hadrosaurs) or well protected against attack (the horned ceratopsians and tank-like ankylosaurs); a mixed diet of carrion and live prey seems the likely conclusion.

The giant plant-eaters

The first herbivorous dinosaurs, such as *Anchisaurus* and *Plateosaurus*, date from Late Triassic rocks, which are mainly younger than those containing the first carnivorous dinosaurs. Both of these herbivores show an advance over the theropods in that they could walk on all fours as well as on their hind legs. Indeed, this ability permitted *Plateosaurus* and its descendants to achieve great size. These Late Triassic and Early Jurassic, medium-sized to large herbivores — the prosauropods — have small heads, long necks and short teeth, all of which foreshadow the giant sauropods which descended from them in the Jurassic.

There has been some debate recently about prosauropod diets. It is accepted that prosauropods were descended from carnivorous ancestors, and it has been suggested that they too might have been at least partially carnivorous. They had powerful jaws, sharp teeth, massive thumb claws and strong limbs. Some specimens have been found associated with clearly carnivorous teeth. However, this evidence has been denied as merely circumstantial by Dr Peter Galton of the University of Bridgeport, Connec-

ticut, in a 1986 review of the problem. All the skeletal features of the prosauropods are directed to plant-eating. The teeth are those of a herbivore, the large claw was probably used to rake up leaves and in fighting, and the relative abundance of prosauropods such as *Plateosaurus*, which dominates the communities of its time, shows that they were the antelopes of their day (animal communities always contain more plant-eaters than meat-eaters, for obvious reasons of supply and demand). The theropod-like teeth found in association with the skeletons, Galton argued, did not belong to the prosauropods but to theropods feeding on them, and they were odd teeth that snapped off in the haste to crunch up a tasty joint.

During the middle Jurassic the prosauropods gave way, in stages, to the mighty sauropods — the group that contained the dominant herbivores of the Late Jurassic. Creatures such as *Brachiosaurus* were the largest land animals of all time. The statistics speak for themselves: 22.5 metres long, 12 metres tall, and 78 tonnes estimated weight. The

The early Chinese prosauropod Lufengosaurus, *mounted in an upright pose (left). It stood like this to feed on tree branches, but walked on all fours.*

The skull of Camarasaurus *(right), a relative, has the nostrils on top of the head and peg-like teeth in the jaws.*

ANCHISAURUS

Anchisaurus, *one of the earliest prosauropods, is known from partial skeletons from various regions of North America and from southern Africa.* Anchisaurus *was obviously a biped, only two and a half metres long, and it fed on low plants. Later relatives of* Anchisaurus, *like* Plateosaurus, *were considerably larger and they reverted to a four-legged posture at times; the latter was typical of their descendants, the giant sauropods.* Anchisaurus *had blunt diamond-shaped teeth lining its jaws, ideal for dealing with leaves. The first skeleton was found in Connecticut in 1818, which probably makes it the first dinosaur to be discovered in North America.*

SALTASAURUS

Saltasaurus, *found in Argentina in 1980, was one of the last surviving sauropods. The group died out in most places after the Late Jurassic, but a few lived on for 80 million years or more into the Late Cretaceous.* Saltasaurus *had unusual armoured bony plates set into its skin. There were large irregular plates up to 10 centimetres in diameter set in a matrix of smaller five millimetre-wide plates.*

less well-known brachiosaurs, *Supersaurus* and *Ultrasaurus*, may have been even larger — up to 17 metres tall and 100 tonnes in weight. These figures are close to the theoretical maximum size for a land animal that would not simply sink into the ground under its own weight. Any larger than this, and a four-legged animal would have had such treetrunk-like legs that they could not have operated in walking!

Brachiosaurus is known from partial skeletons discovered in Colorado and Utah in the United States, as well as from spectacular finds made by Werner Janensch on the famous East African excavations in 1907-1912 at Tendaguru, in what is now Tanzania. He directed hundreds of helpers, who dug up and plastered hundreds of tonnes of bones which were carried on their heads over many kilometres to the nearest ports for shipment to Germany. The mounted skeleton in the Humboldt Museum, East Berlin, must surely be one of the best dinosaur exhibits in the world.

Brachiosaurus had very long forelimbs, and its neck vertebrae show that the neck could be hoisted vertically. This great reptilian "giraffe" presumably fed on leaves from the tops of tall trees, well beyond the reach of other ground-dwelling animals. However, the vast bulk and long neck of *Brachiosaurus* pose a variety of key problems. How could it eat enough to keep going, especially in view of its tiny head, how could it pump blood some 8 metres or more from heart to head? And how could it move the massive weight of its neck?

At one time, the sauropods were reconstructed as sluggish swamp-dwelling, overgrown salamanders that mumbled away at soft waterside plants and barely moved. The neck slithered about and its arc-like motions sufficed to gather enough food. This view is unlikely to be correct since the sauropods had strong legs, like those of an elephant, but proportionately larger, and hence they were

HETERODONTOSAURUS

Heterodontosaurus was a small plant-eater, just over one metre in total length. It was capable of rapid movement, as shown by the strong legs, in order to escape from predatory theropods. Specimens of Heterodontosaurus *were collected in southern Africa in the 1960s in Lower Jurassic sediments, dating from 200 million years ago. This dinosaur seems to be near the root of ornithopod evolution, as an early ancestor of* Iguanodon *and the duckbills.*

capable of walking. In addition, the large food requirements of a sauropod meant that it would have to move fair distances over land, as elephants do today, when it had exhausted the supply of food in one place.

In 1971 Dr Robert Bakker, then of Yale University, published a series of heretical suggestions. He argued that the sauropods were fully adapted to living on land, that they could gallop as fast as any modern rhinoceros, and that most could rear up on their hind legs when fighting or feeding. Most palaeontologists viewed these ideas as rather "over-the-top", but Bakker's arguments convinced many that the sauropods were, at least, more than giant slugs. Detailed analyses of the biomechanical properties of their limbs, limb bones and footprints show that the large sauropods could not have run. They may have ambled at a quick human walking speed; but any faster, and their legs would have broken (the faster an animal runs, the more

impact stress is generated through the bones as the feet hit the ground). Such sauropods could feed on water plants or browse in trees hoisting their heads high into the foliage. However, they probably did this for moments only, otherwise the blood supply to the brain would diminish or cease. Calculations of the blood pressure and size of heart required to pump blood straight upwards for eight or more metres show that such a posture was impossible in a sustained fashion. However, sauropods had very small brains, and a minute or two without fresh blood may not have been any great hardship!

Ornithopod evolution

The ornithischians arose long after the theropods and prosauropods — according to some analyses, possibly as late as the beginning of the Jurassic, some 25 million years after the origin of the dinosaurs. However, other palaeontologists, such as Dr Paul Sereno of the University of Chicago, believe that there were very early ornithischians, such as *Pisanosaurus*, which lived at the same time as *Coelophysis*. The only known skeleton of this dinosaur, from Brazil, is incomplete but it does shows characteristic low, triangular-crowned teeth arranged as in later ornithischians. In addition the teeth are set inwards on the jaw, leaving a rather broad shelf on the outside — a sure sign that *Pisanosaurus* had fleshy cheeks. The saurischian dinosaurs, theropods and sauropodomorphs did not have cheeks, whereas ornithischians did; this may be one of the keys to their success.

Cheeks are pouches of skin on either side of the back teeth. They are used to retain food, particularly plant food, while it is being processed. If a cow bites off some grass, this is passed back into the cheek region for grinding; the cheeks retain any pieces cut off outside the teeth. As a lizard bites a leaf, the fragments on either side of its tooth rows drop off when it cuts through them. This wasteful practice was avoided independently, in both ornithischians and mammals, by the evolution of cheeks.

The earliest well-known ornithischians are ornithopods such as *Heterodontosaurus* from the Early Jurassic of South Africa. Unusually, this moderate-sized biped had differentiated teeth: two cutting incisors, a long canine, and about 12 cheek teeth along each jaw (hence its name, which

The skull (below) of Heterodontosaurus, *an early ornithopod. This unusual plant-eating dinosaur has fangs which may have been used in pre-mating fights between males.*

means "different tooth reptile"). Most reptiles, including most dinosaurs, had teeth which varied little in shape or function from the front to the back of the jaw. It is not clear why *Heterodontosaurus* had differentiated teeth, but the canines may have been used as males fought each other for mates. The incisors were adapted for snipping off vegetation and the cheek teeth for chewing it, as in mammals.

Chewing is something that only mammals can do properly today, but the ornithopod dinosaurs managed to chew as well. Chewing is the breaking down of tough food to small pieces by sideways and backwards-and-forwards grinding movements. In mammals, this is done by the cheek teeth (premolars and molars); the jaw joint is very flexible, to allow the complex circular and sawing motions required. In reptiles, birds and other vertebrates, the jaw joint is little more than a hinge. It can allow only simple up-and-down motions, with no sawing or rotation. Initially, ornithopods faced many of these constraints at their jaw hinges, but they developed extra joints to allow chewing. This happened in two ways, one in *Heterodontosaurus* and a second in all other ornithopods.

The ability to chew

Heterodontosaurus had an extra ball-and-socket joint at the front of its lower jaw, and the jaws rocked in and out as they moved up and down. The normal jaw hinge was fixed at the back, and the pointed lower beak (the predentary part of the jaw) was fixed at the front, while the middle segments of the jaws flapped in and out passively during normal up-and-down movements. In other ornithopods, the lower jaw was a firm unit, but the skull had mobile sides. New joints evolved along the sides of the snout to the eye sockets, and round the back of the cheek region, as well as across the palate. As the lower jaw closed against the teeth of the upper jaw, the cheek portions of the skull moved out by a centimetre or so, producing a lateral grinding movement between upper and lower teeth. As the jaw moved down, the cheeks flapped in, and an opposite lateral grinding movement occurred. Hence, the normal reptilian hinge joint was transformed by these secondary "pleurokinetic" joints into a complex chewing mechanism. The biomechanical details of ornithopod jaws are currently being worked out by Dr David Norman of the Nature Conservancy Council, Peterborough, England, and Dr David Weishampel of the Johns Hopkins University, Baltimore, Maryland. Such studies involve close examination of well-preserved skulls and teeth, computerized biomechanical modelling and working scale models.

The ornithopods had limited success in the Jurassic.

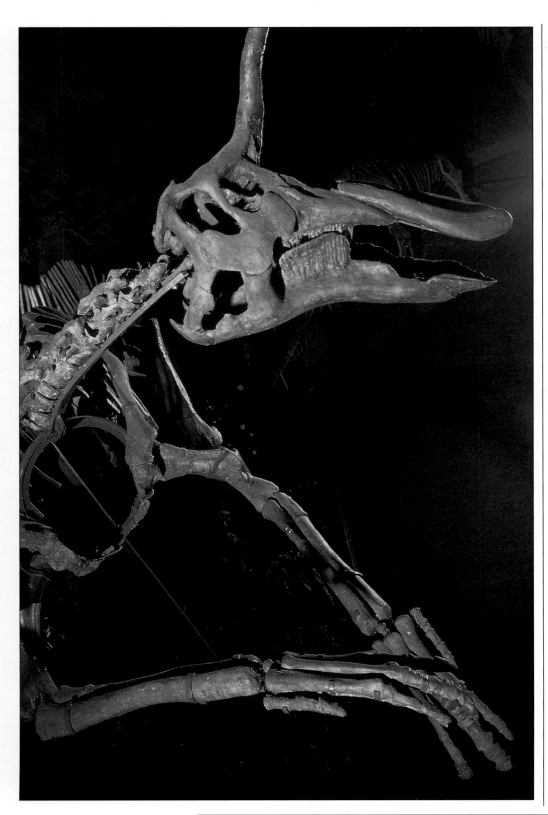

Types such as *Dryosaurus* in Africa and North America were agile, bipedal plant-eaters that may have fed on tougher plants than those consumed by the dominant sauropods. They were fleet of foot, to escape the attention of theropods like *Allosaurus*.

The sauropods declined in importance in the Cretaceous, although some, like *Saltasaurus*, lived on to the end of this time, particularly in South America. The ornithopods, however, diversified dramatically throughout the Cretaceous. Their success is probably due to their efficient chewing mechanism, which the sauropods lacked. It may also relate to major changes that were taking place among the plants.

In the Jurassic, subtropical forests of conifers, bennettitaleans, cycads and ginkgos covered most of the dinosaur lands. Sauropods and stegosaurs fed high in the branches of the trees.

These groups of plants started to decline during the Early Cretaceous, and the bennettitaleans began to die out. The others survive today, but only the conifers are abundant. New flowering plants, the angiosperms, appeared and increasingly took over the land surface of the Earth. Angiosperms include most terrestrial plants today: cabbages, oaks, daffodils and grasses, and it seems hard to imagine a world without them.

The ornithopods arose and radiated in line with the angiosperms. Whether the ornithopods or the angiosperms came first is hard to say. Evidence for both views has been put forward recently: that the angiosperms led to the success of the ornithopods, and vice versa.

The latter argument puts forward the view that ornithopods grazed low, and consumed seedlings of the primitive groups of plants, thus clearing the way for the more rapidly seeding angiosperms. This did not happen when the sauropods were the main herbivores, since they browsed leaves from high in trees, and left the conifer and cycad seedlings alone. On the evidence that exists at present, who can say which view is correct?

The Early Cretaceous radiation of ornithopods included

The front part of a skeleton of the hadrosaur Tsintaosaurus *shows the batteries of teeth (left). During its life, a hadrosaur grew many sets of teeth, which permitted these advanced ornithopods to eat quantities of tough plants.*

The skeleton of **Iguanodon** *went on show for the first time in Brussels, Belgium, in 1883 (above). Several complete skeletons had just been found in a nearby coal mine.*

The skeleton of **Camptosaurus** *(above), a Late Jurassic ornithopod known from North America and Europe. This plant-eater reached seven metres in length.*

Iguanodon *had an unusual hand (right), with a pointed thumb spike (1), possibly used in defence. The other fingers had small hooves (2) instead of claws, showing that the hand was used in locomotion. The wrist bones were fused (3) for added strength.*

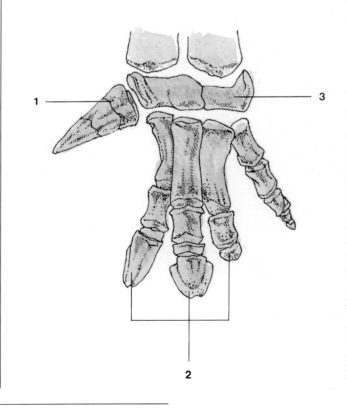

the iguanodontids. They had horse-like heads, a bony cropping plate at the front of the mouth (as in sheep) and rows of close-set, grinding cheek teeth. All were moderate to large bipeds, capable of rapid running and probably feeding in large herds. *Iguanodon* itself had a sharp thumb claw which it used in self-defence and in male-versus-male fighting. The other fingers had small hooves instead of claws, showing that the hand was used in locomotion. The wrist bones were fused for added strength. One of the most exciting dinosaur discoveries concerned *Iguanodon*. In 1878 at Bernissart in Belgium, a group of miners found dinosaur remains in a coalfield. Subsequent excavations unearthed the remains of 39 *Iguanodon* skeletons.

A major reappraisal of the biology of these animals has taken place recently. In 1970, Dr Peter Galton presented a forceful argument that palaeontologists had misunder-

stood the posture of *Iguanodon* for years. Older reconstructions show this dinosaur in "kangaroo pose", that is, with the body nearly vertical and the tail acting as a kind of third leg, tripod fashion. The beast was even pictured waddling along in this upright posture. But Galton noted that the hip girdle was located about the animal's centre of gravity, and the body balanced best if the backbone was held horizontal, with the heavy tail sticking out straight behind and the trunk and head ranged in front. The curvature of the backbone in the anterior trunk and neck region confirmed this view, since there was an S-shaped bend to position the head in a forward-looking direction when the back was held horizontally. In addition, the tails of many ornithopods are strengthened with stiff, bony rods along their sides. Evidently the tail was held out, rigid and unbending, only possible if it acts as a horizontal balancing rod.

OURANOSAURUS

Ouranosaurus, *a close relative of* Iguanodon, *has a very similar skeleton, apart from the remarkable sail on its back. The sail is supported by elongated neural spines on the vertebrae of the back, and it may have had a thermoregulatory function, as proposed for the unrelated pelycosaurs of 140 million years earlier.* Ouranosaurus *reached seven metres in length. Skeletons were first collected in Niger, North Africa, in the early 1970s.*

SKULLS AND JAWS

Dinosaur skulls exhibit a variety of shapes and sizes. The shapes were largely determined by their role in feeding, the snout length, jaw depth, jaw joint, and tooth shape, size and spacing all depending on diet. Indeed, dinosaur skulls give a great deal of information. The skull shapes and teeth of theropods (opposite page) changed less than those of the herbivorous dinosaurs. Even though *Deinonychus*, *Allosaurus* and *Tyrannosaurus* were of very different sizes and lived at different times, their jaw shapes and teeth were similar. The herbivorous sauropodomorphs (this page) had a variety of skull shapes. Most successful herbivorous dinosaurs were the ornithopods (far right, opposite page) who had a characteristic method of chewing. These dinosaurs had batteries of teeth growing up continuously from below.

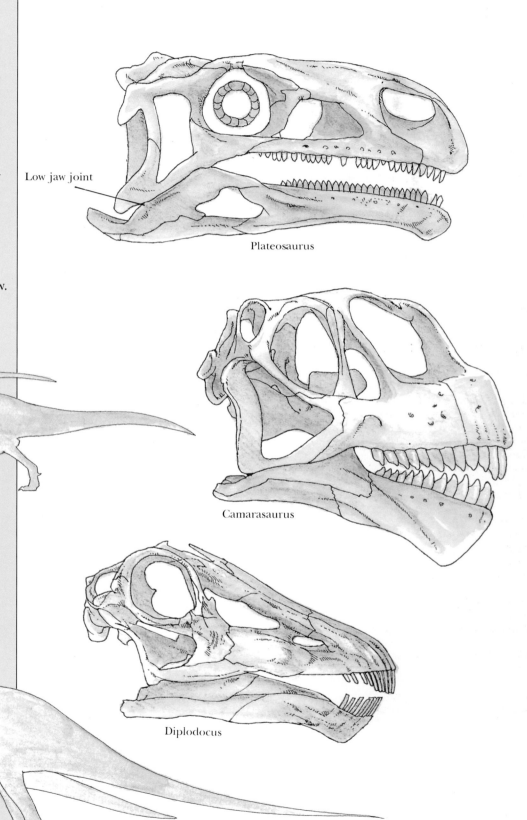

Low jaw joint

Plateosaurus

Camarasaurus

Diplodocus

Above: Some carnivorous theropods, such as Deinonychus *(1), were human-sized, while others, such as* Tyrannosaurus *(2) and* Allosaurus *(3) were larger.*

Below: The sauropodomorphs Plateosaurus *(1),* Diplodocus *(2), and* Camarasaurus *(3) were all larger than humans.*

Plateosaurus, *had primitively long skulls, as in ancestral archosaurs. The leaf-shaped teeth, which were spaced along the long, horse-like jaws, cut the vegetation like a weak pair of scissors. The jaw joint was below the level of the tooth row, an adaptation commonly used to increase the power of the jaw closure.*

The later sauropods, such as Camarasaurus *and* Diplodocus, *had greatly modified skulls in which the nostrils have moved back to the top of the skull, the snout has shortened, and the teeth are concentrated at the front of the mouth. In this position, they can have been used only for nipping off vegetation, rather than for cutting it up further back in the mouth.*

Allosaurus, *from the Late Jurassic of North America, had a deep jaw bone, which indicates powerful jaw muscles. The recurved teeth were ideal for tearing flesh, and their backwards curve enabled them to hang on to struggling prey.*

The smaller Deinonychus *had a narrower jaw with an obvious large opening, the mandibular fenestra, in the side. Its function is unknown.*

The giant Tyrannosaurus, *the largest terrestrial carnivore of all time, had a powerful deep lower jaw. There was an extra joint half way along the lower jaw which allowed* Tyrannosaurus *to open its mouth rather more widely in order to deal with a large prey.*

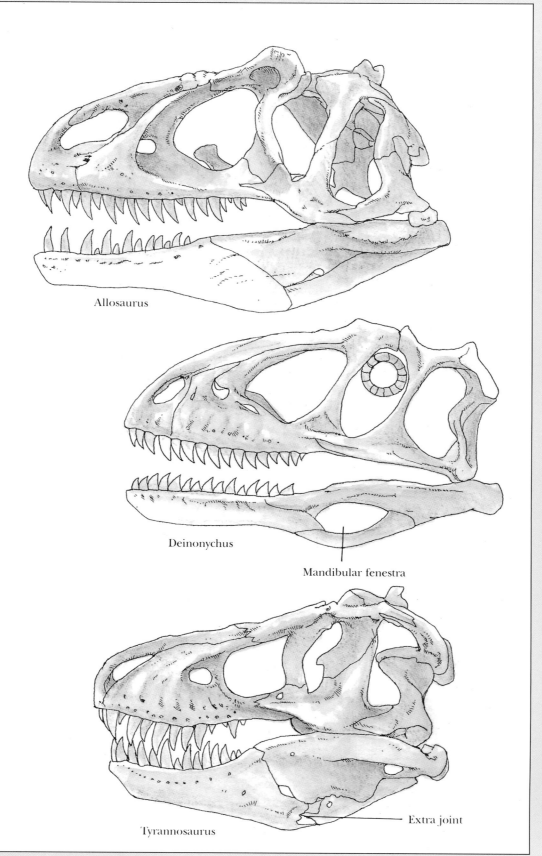

Allosaurus

Deinonychus

Mandibular fenestra

Tyrannosaurus

Extra joint

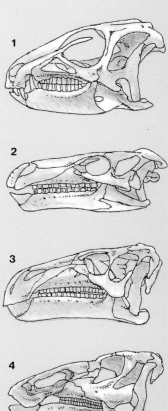

1

2

3

4

The herbivorous ornithopods like Heterodontosaurus *(1) fed on a varied diet of leaves. The jaws were arranged for a kind of "chewing", a unique feature. The lower jaws of* Heterodontosaurus *rotated in and out as they opened and closed to produce sideways chewing movements.*
In later ornithopods, such as Camptosaurus *(2),* Iguanodon *(3) and* Edmontosaurus *(4), the chewing motion was produced in a different way: the lower jaws were held rigid during a jaw cycle, but the cheek region of the skull flapped in and out, producing a sideways grinding of the teeth.*

Hadrosaur biology

The hadrosaurs, or duckbilled dinosaurs, ruled the Late Cretaceous landscapes as antelopes do today in Africa. Most hadrosaurs had similar bodies, the dozens of species being distinguished on the basis of their head crests. Many hadrosaurs had unadorned heads, but others had a variety of bumps, spikes, tubes and ridges above and behind the eyes. In every case, the crests are made from backward extensions of the premaxillae and nasals — the bones that lie on top of the snout, between the nostrils and the eye sockets. A cross-section of a hadrosaur skull shows that the nasal cavity extends right to the ends of the crest, however convoluted it may be. Hence, air is drawn in through the nostrils, passes up, into and through the crest, and then back down again to the throat and lungs. Air is breathed out along the same tortuous route.

At one time, it was thought that the crests were aqualungs or perhaps snorkels; the hadrosaurs were interpreted as highly aquatic, with dabbling duck-like bills and webbed feet. They could supposedly hold sufficient air in the crest for a short dive, or even use it as a snorkel — (particularly in *Parasaurolophus,* which had a long, tube-like crest. However, the crest was not open at the tip and so could not have operated like a snorkel. Moreover, the overall capacity of a crest was far too small to make it of any use as an aqualung for such a large animal. Current opinion is that the hadrosaurs were essentially terrestrial animals that often frequented dry forested areas, feeding on tough leaves which they ground with their batteries of powerful teeth.

What were the crests for, then? It seems clear that they were recognition signals, to distinguish between species

The crested hadrosaur Saurolophus angustirostris *from North America (left). This duck-billed, plant-eating ornithopod grew up to 12 metres in length as an adult, and close relatives are known from central Asia. The crest was an extension of the nasal and frontal bones of the skull, and it might have allowed* Saurolophus *to bellow.*

MAIASAURA

Maiasaura, *or "good mother reptile", was named in 1979 from several skeletons found in Montana. This crestless hadrosaur is well known since it was found in association with its nest, eggs, and young.* Maiasaura *laid between 10 and 30 eggs in a large earth nest on the ground. It seems that the parents cared for the hatchlings until they were able to forage for themselves.*

YOUNG AND OLD SKULLS

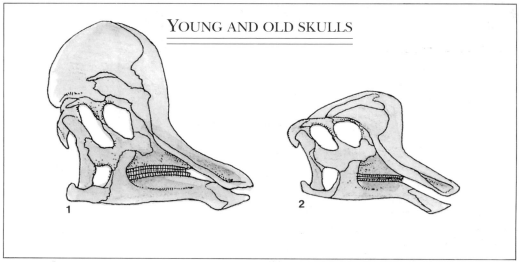

1

2

Crests varied between adult and juvenile hadrosaurs (left). An adult Corythosaurus *(1) had a relatively larger crest than a juvenile (2).*

and possibly between sexes. The shape of the crest told a hadrosaur whether another animal was of the same species, and hence whether it was worth interacting with in some way. Further, it has now been shown that many of the crests show "sexual dimorphism": within one hadrosaur type, half the fossil population had crests of one shape while the other half had crests that were similar but different in some way — smaller, say. These species and sexual recognition functions were evidently enhanced by sounds. Work by Dr David Weishampel, published in 1983, showed that the complex windings of the nasal passages in some hadrosaur crests mimicked various wind instruments. He found that he could obtain a variety of bellows and squeaks from scale models of hadrosaur nasal crests, and postulated that each sex of each species made a characteristic hooting or trumpeting noise. The Late Cretaceous landscape of Alberta must have been the equal of any noisy jungle!

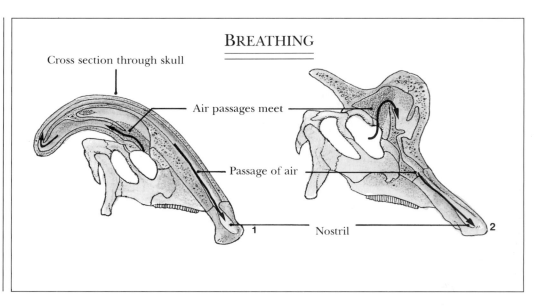

BREATHING

Cross section through skull

Air passages meet

Passage of air

Nostril

1

2

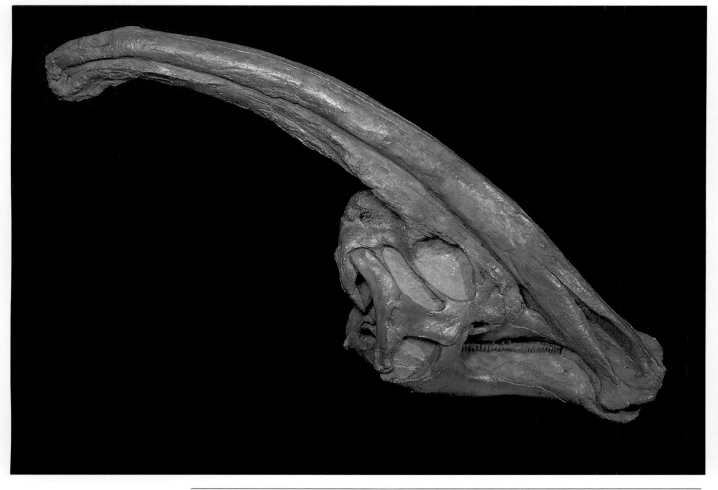

Above: Parasaurolophus walkeri, *the most spectacular species of crested hadrosaur (1). At one time it was thought that the crest was used as a snorkel, but in fact it was closed at the end. On breathing out, air passed from the throat into the base of the crest, up the tubes and down the main tube to the nostrils.* Lambeosaurus *(2) has a very different crest shape, but the nasal passages were similar.*

The skull of **Parasaurolophus Walkeri** *(left) one of the most extremely modified hadrosaur skulls. The crest is made out of the nasal and frontal bones which have grown backwards and have fused together into a tubular structure.*

HADROSAUR EVOLUTION

Hadrosaur evolution is charted by the shapes of their crests. An early crestless form give rise to the great diversity. The crests are made from the nasal and frontal bones.

Hadrosaur skulls. The female (1) and male (2) skulls of Parasaurolophus walkeri *show sexual differences in the shape of their spectacular crests. The same is true of the female (3) and male (4)* Lambeosaurus *with their unusual two-part crests.*

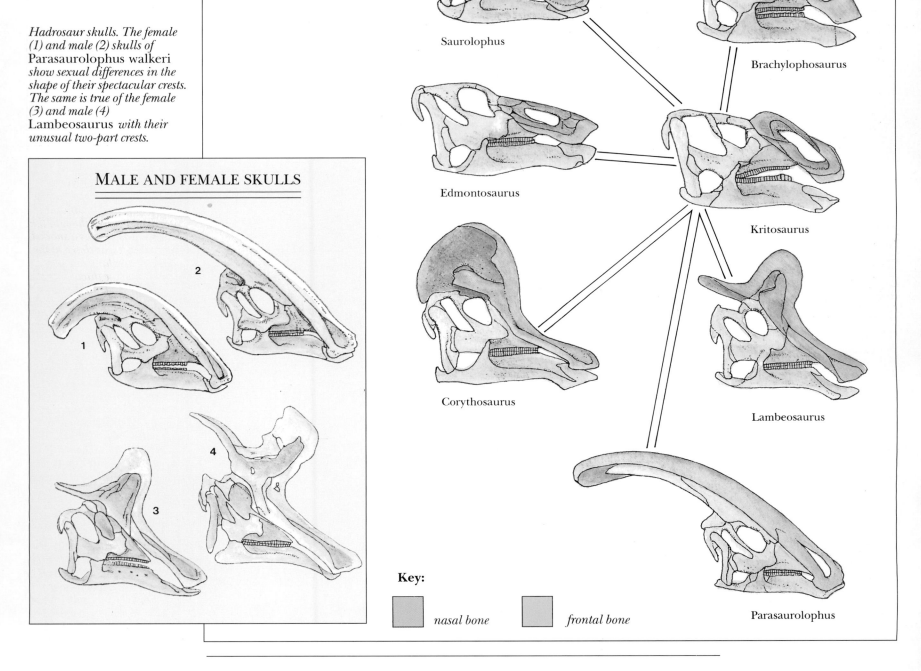

MALE AND FEMALE SKULLS

Saurolophus

Brachylophosaurus

Edmontosaurus

Kritosaurus

Corythosaurus

Lambeosaurus

Parasaurolophus

Key:

nasal bone   frontal bone

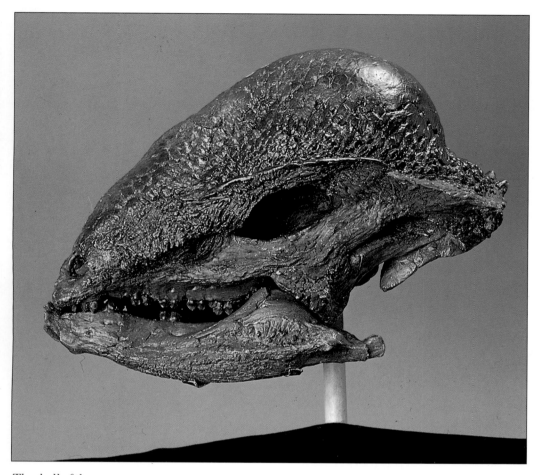

The pachycephalosaurs

Pachycephalosaurs (literally "thick-headed reptiles") are a poorly known group from the Late Cretaceous of North America and Mongolia. That is, poorly known until recently, when more complete skeletons have been found. Most pachycephalosaurs are known only from their massively thickened skull roofs, which can be 20 centimetres thick in a 60-centimetres-long skull. The pachycephalosaur body resembles an iguanodontid, but the head is the unique feature. Ringed with spines and knobs of bone, the frontal and parietal bones swell into a massive bulge above and behind the eyes. This is no hadrosaur crest, containing delicate nasal passages, but strengthened bone designed for one purpose, namely battering.

The head-battering feature of pachycephalosaur behaviour was proposed by Dr Peter Galton in 1970, when he argued that animals like *Stegoceras* were the Cretaceous equivalent of sheep or buffalo. The males had tougher cranial domes than the females, and they engaged in battering contests to win mates.

As in modern mountain sheep and cattle, the blows were probably powerful enough to kill any other animal, but the skull of a rival pachycephalosaur was so reinforced that very little damage ensued. It was compact and solid below the dome, so that the force of impact was dissipated around the sides and to the neck without causing a fracture. The neck, shoulders and hip girdles were also heavily constructed in order to absorb the force.

The skull of the pachycephalosaur Stegoceras *(above) is dominated by the high skull roof. This is made from greatly thickened bone and surrounded by small, irregular, bony knobs.*

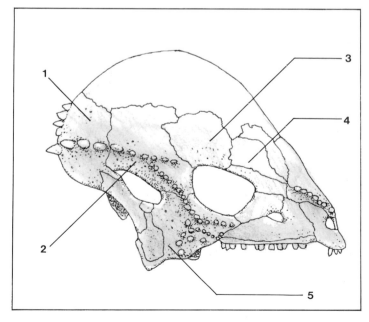

The unusual skull of the pachycephalosaur (left) is made from the "distorted" bones of a normal ornithopod skull. The main dome is surrounded by knobs on the squamosal (1) and postorbital (2) bones. Two extra supraorbital bones (3, 4) are inserted over the eye socket. The jugal (5) also bears knobs.

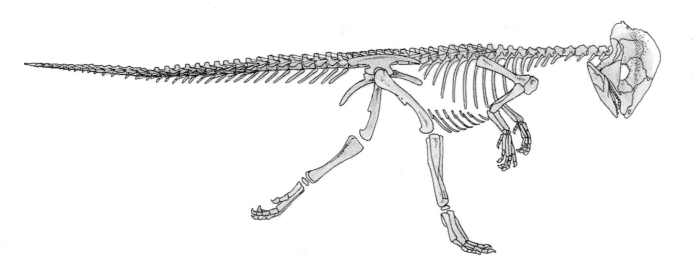

The whole pachycephalosaur skeleton was modified for head-butting (left). The backbone and hip bones were strengthened to absorb impact, and the powerful limbs allowed the opponents to build up considerable speed before they clashed.

STEGOCERAS

Stegoceras *was a medium-sized pachycephalosaur, about two metres long. It was named in 1902 on the basis of two skull fragments, but a partial skeleton was discovered in the year 1920. Most pachycephalosaurs are known only from their massively thickened skull roofs, so the* Stegoceras *partial skeleton was important in allowing an* assessment of their way of life. It is likely that the males used their massively thickened skulls in territorial or mating head-butting contests.

The horn-faced ceratopsians

Another Late Cretaceous group, closely related to the pachycephalosaurs, and more distantly to the ornithopods, were the ceratopsians. Their evolution has been very well documented.

The earliest member of the group, *Psittacosaurus*, seems to be a perfect intermediate stage, being a facultative biped (it could walk on its hind legs or on all fours at will), and having only the merest hints of later ceratopsian specialities. The jaws were deep and there was a parrot-like beak at the front — hence the name, meaning "parrot reptile". The head was also rather triangular in plan view, another characteristic of the group. The toothless beak at the front of the jaws was used to snip up tough plants, and they were chewed by batteries of cheek teeth. Many *Psittacosaurus* remains have been found, most notably in Mongolia, including whole skeletons.

The skull of Protoceratops *(right), an early ceratopsian from Mongolia, bears a clear frill, but the face horns are barely developed. There is a thickening over the snout, but no horn.*

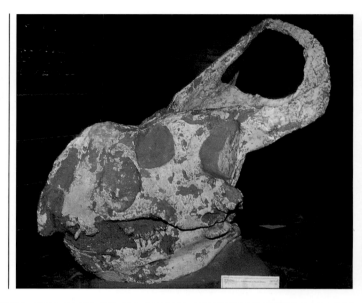

PSITTACOSAURUS

Psittacosaurus *was the first ceratopsian, or horned, dinosaur. It is clearly only slightly modified from a typical ornithopod such as* Iguanodon, *but it has the horny beak and thickend nasal region of the skull seen in later ceratopsians. The front of the jaws was a toothless beak used to snip up tough plants, and these were chewed by batteries of cheek teeth.*

Triceratops *has a broad, bony frill at the back of the skull (right) which extended over the shoulder region. Massive jaw muscles attached to the wide upper surface of the frill, and it also provided some protection.*

Triceratops, *the best-known horned dinosaur (below). The pattern of blood vessel canals on the surface of the horn bones and frill indicates that these were covered with skin in life. The limbs are built to support the weight of the heavy animal, but also for speed.*

Many fossils, from Mongolia and North America in particular, show how the two key ceratopsian features evolved. The skull bones on top of the snout and above the eyes progressively formed bumps, and then horns, which were probably used in defence. In later ceratopsians, such as *Triceratops*, the bony projections were covered with horn (keratin) sheaths, just like the horny coverings to the horns of sheep and cattle.

The second ceratopsian feature is the neck frill, a backwards extension of the parietal and squamosal bones at the back of the skull. These skull bones anchor some of the key jaw-closing muscles. As they grew backwards in the ceratopsians, the jaw muscles presumably went with them and lengthened, so changing the mechanics of the jaw action, to allow a powerful bite.

Ceratopsians show great variety in the number and distribution of their horns, and in the shape of the frill. Some have one rhinoceros-like snout horn, others possess three (including *Triceratops*) while others sport five. The frill may be rounded or square, and smooth or surrounded by knobs of bone, or long spikes. Such structures, as with the hadrosaur crests, may have served as species and sexual recognition features, as well as in defence.

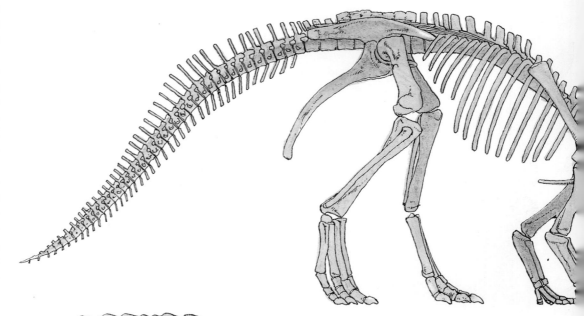

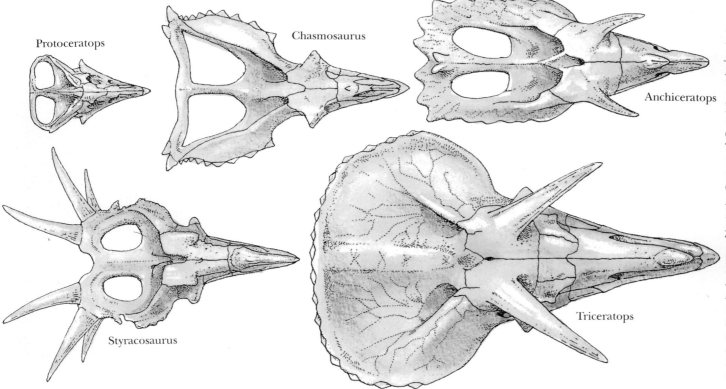

Protoceratops

Chasmosaurus

Anchiceratops

Styracosaurus

Triceratops

Evolution of the ceratopsian skulls followed four main lines from Protoceratops. *One progressed to* Styracosaurus, *with multiple spines on its frill; the second to the hornless* Leptoceratops; *the third through* Brachyceratops *and* Centrosaurus *to* Triceratops, *the short-frilled lineage; and the fourth involved long-frilled forms,* Chasmosaurus, Anchiceratops, Pentaceratops, Arrhinoceratops *and* Torosaurus, *this last one with a head as long as a car. Plan views of ceratopsian skulls (left) show the relative size of the bony neck frill and the variable array of horns in each species. The frill is an outgrowth of two of the bones at the back of the skull, and the horns are bony cores, covered with horn.*

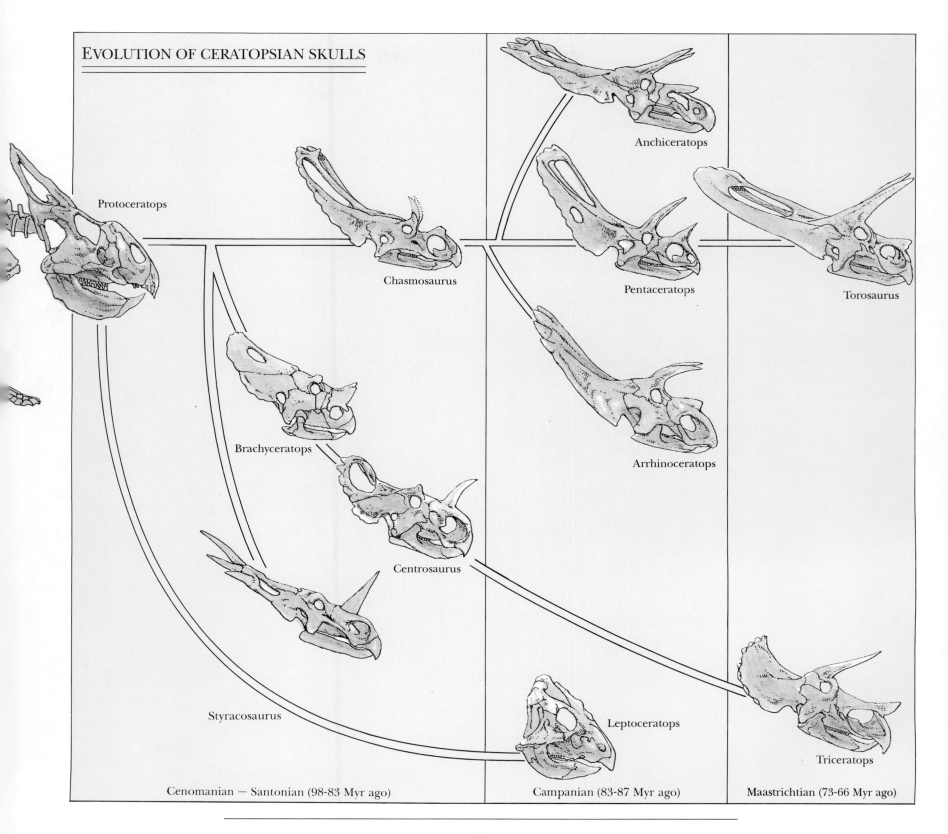

EVOLUTION OF CERATOPSIAN SKULLS

Protoceratops

Chasmosaurus

Anchiceratops

Pentaceratops

Torosaurus

Brachyceratops

Arrhinoceratops

Centrosaurus

Styracosaurus

Leptoceratops

Triceratops

Cenomanian — Santonian (98-83 Myr ago)

Campanian (83-87 Myr ago)

Maastrichtian (73-66 Myr ago)

The thyreophorans: stegosaurs and ankylosaurs

New phylogenies of the ornithischian dinosaurs agree in pairing the plated stegosaurs and ankylosaurs together, as thyreophorans. They branched from the ornithopods, pachycephalosaurs and ceratopsians in the Early Jurassic, according to Dr Paul Sereno's 1986 revision of ornithischian evolution. Even so, neither group really made a showing until the Late Jurassic, and the ankylosaurs' heyday was mainly in the Late Cretaceous, some 120 million years after their origin.

The stegosaurs form part of the sauropod-stegosaur herbivore community that dominated the Late Jurassic. They had a variety of plates and spines arrayed over the neck, back, hips and tail. *Kentrosaurus* from East Africa had mainly spines, while the well-known *Stegosaurus* itself had

great lozenge-shaped plates set upright along its back, as well as four spikes at the end of its tail. The tail spikes were probably defensive, discouraging attacks by predators such as *Allosaurus*, but what of the back-plates?

The first problem is to establish how the plates were arranged. In early reconstructions of *Stegosaurus* they were set in a single row, like a picket fence, from neck to tail. Next, the double-alternating-rows version prevailed. One unusual proposal was that the plates were flat, like roof tiles, forming a kind of carapace over the back. Then, in 1986, Stephen Czerkas went full circle and proposed that the picket fence model was correct after all.

Why cannot palaeontologists decide on such a fundamental anatomical point? The fact is that the plates, although made of bone, were not part of the normal ske-

The early stegosaur Tuojiangosaurus *(right) has smaller plates and spines than* Stegosaurus. *The body shape is similar, as are the tiny skull and the broad, plate-like ilium (upper hip bone).*

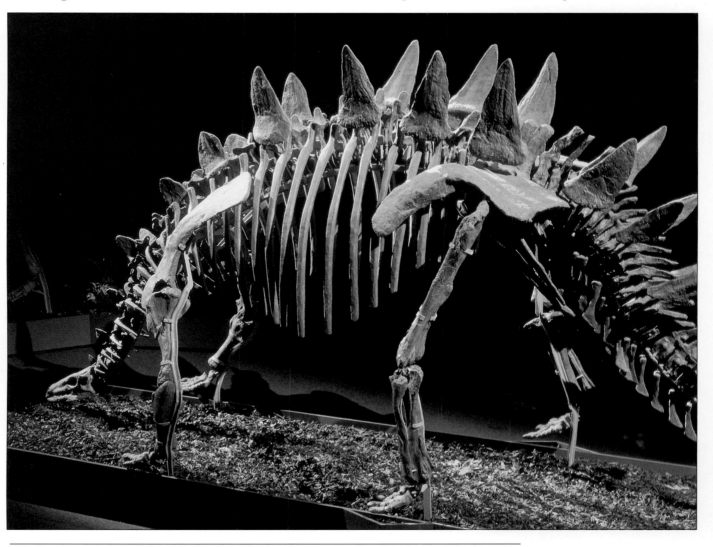

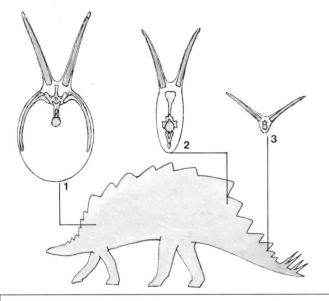

The bony plates on the back of Stegosaurus *vary in size and shape from the neck to the tail (right). The plates in the middle of the back (1) are tall and widely spaced, those at the base of the tail (2) are smaller, while the last few on the tail (3) are broadly spreading spines.*

leton. They were dermal bones, like the bony scutes of a crocodile, and they had no direct connection with the backbone. Therefore they can be arranged in any whimsical way that strikes the palaeontologist's fancy. The horizontal plate model was disproved by a microscopic examination of their cross-sections, carried out in 1984. It showed that tendinous fibres entered the bone tissue at angles concomitant with a vertical placement. Czerkas noted that the collector's surviving notes associated with the best *Stegosaurus* skeletons, found over 100 years ago, suggested that the two-row model depended on adding extra back plates from several individuals. In other words, the original skeletons only had enough plates for a single row down the middle of the back.

Why were the plates there at all? They would certainly

STEGOSAURUS

Stegosaurus, *the best-known armoured dinosaur, reached seven and a half metres in length. Named in 1877, its skeletons have now been found in many parts of the midwestern United States. The plates on the back were made from bone but were not attached to the skeleton, being merely rooted in the skin and muscles.* Stegosaurus *walked on all fours, but it could have reared up to feed in trees.*

have prevented a predator biting *Stegosaurus* on the back, but the vulnerable flanks were left unprotected. A thermoregulatory function seems more likely — control of body temperature. In life, the plates were probably covered by massive blood vessels (shown by grooves in the bone), and hence by skin too. This was an effective radiator for heat-exchange with the environment. When the animal's blood was cool, it would absorb heat from the sun as it coursed over the exposed plates and then passed throughout the body. If *Stegosaurus* overheated at midday, the dinosaur could stand in a breeze and lose excess warmth through the back fins.

The ankylosaurs were the most heavily armoured dinosaurs, being covered from head to tail in a carapace of small bony plates set in the skin. The covering was as efficient as that of a turtle. Typical ankylosaurs, like *Ankylosaurus* itself, had extra sheets of bone connected to the skull roof, so that the head was extremely well armoured. The carapace covered the neck. back and tail, and the small bony plates were interspersed with long spines around the sides. When attacked by *Tyrannosaurus,* an ankylosaur probably tucked its limbs underneath its body and so weathered any kicking or biting. In addition, *Ankylosaurus* had a massive bony knob on the end of its tail, formed by the fusion of the last caudal vertebrae. This could have been swung with considerable force and deadly accuracy at any predator. Remember that the ankylosaurs were far from turtle-like in size; *Ankylosaurus* was six metres long, the size of a small army tank, and it was virtually impregnable to attack.

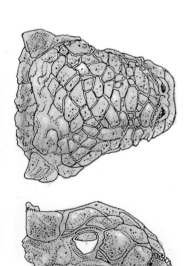

The skull of the ankylosaur **Euoplocephalus** *seen from above (top) and the side (above). The nostrils are nearly hidden beneath bone, and bony plates cover the eye sockets. There is even a bony eyelid.*

ANKYLOSAURUS

Ankylosaurus, *the living tank of Late Cretaceous times, about 70 million years ago. It may look broadly like a turtle, but it was up to 17 metres long, and would have been a formidable dinosaur for* Tyrannosaurus *to attack.* Ankylosaurus *had strong feet and limbs built for speed. Its back was armoured by a mesh of bony plates set in the skin, and the tail bore a "club" at the end which could be wielded with some force.*

The Mongolian ankylosaurid Talarurus, *mounted in a rather sprawling posture. When it ran, it probably tucked its limbs close in beneath the body. The broad back was armoured with bony nodules in the skin*

DINOSAURS OF THE EARLY CRETACEOUS

A rainy scene in southern England, 120 million years ago, in a low-lying estuarine area, the Wealden, which extended from Hampshire and the Isle of Wight, over London, to northern France, Belgium and parts of Germany. Extensive meandering stream channels preserve conifer logs, bones and teeth of fish, freshwater turtles, rat-sized mammals, crocodiles and dinosaurs.

The Wealden dinosaurs include rare and little known sauropods (background), as well as the dominant ornithopods *Hypsilophodon* and *Iguanodon* (left). A new discovery, after 170 years of collecting in the Wealden, was the theropod *Baryonyx*. Until then, only fragmentary remains of small theropods had been found. *Baryonyx* was a large animal with a long snout, and it may have fed on fish.

How the world looked in this period

Hypsilophodon *(1), a small ornithopod, was present in much larger numbers than the theropod* Baryonyx *(2). Two species of* Iguanodon *(3, 4) appear to have been the dominant plant-eaters, being* represented by dozens of skeletons. The largest herbivore, Pelorosaurus *(5) is less well known, but must have been large, up to 24 metres long, and well above human scale.*

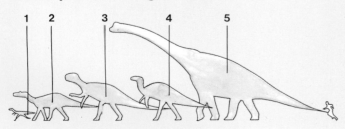

CHAPTER FIVE

UNANSWERED QUESTIONS

Some of the most intriguing questions about dinosaurs are still unanswered. Were they warm-blooded or not? Did they look after their young in any way, or leave them to fend for themselves? Why were the dinosaurs so huge, and what sorts of problems did this cause? Who are their closest living relatives? And, of course, the question that everyone asks: why did they die out?

Were the dinosaurs "warm-blooded"?

Palaeontologists have long puzzled about the thermoregulatory physiology of the dinosaurs — that is, how they controlled the temperature of the body and, by inference, what the metabolic rate was like. (Metabolic rate is the general speed of bodily chemical reactions, which affects activity levels.) Today, birds and mammals are homeotherms: they sustain a high body temperature which does not fluctuate with temperature changes in the surroundings. Animals with variable body temperatures are poikilotherms. But keeping up this constant body temperature is costly. Birds and mammals use up to nine-tenths of their food simply for internal temperature control: food is burned to keep up temperatures in cold conditions, and energy is lost by various means for body cooling when air temperatures soar.

Birds and mammals are endotherms — they have internal temperature control. Lizards, snakes, turtles, amphibians and fishes are ectotherms, with external temperature control; the body temperature generally follows

The life-sized reconstructions of Iguanodon *(above) were put on display in 1853. A grand dinner was held inside the* Iguanodon *model on New Year's Eve 1853-4 to celebrate their completion.*

the air or water temperature quite closely, and hence it fluctuates by a fair amount from midday to midnight. Such creatures may use behavioural techniques to modify their core temperatures, such as basking on a rock to warm up, or hiding in a burrow to cool down, but lizards and crocodiles are largely at the mercy of the environment. The plus side of the equation is that these ectotherms generally need to eat only one-tenth the amount of food required by an endotherm of the same body weight.

Left: Waterhouse Hawkins' workshop at the Crystal Palace, Sydenham, London, in 1853. Life-sized models of Owen's conceptions of Iguanodon *(centre),* Megalosaurus *(right), the amphibian* Mastodonsaurus *(left) and the mammal-like reptile* Dicynodon *(bottom right) are being finished for display.*

Sir Richard Owen (1804-1892), the brilliant Victorian palaeontologist and anatomist (below), who named the Dinosauria. *He was evidently a grim figure who was disliked by most of his contemporaries.*

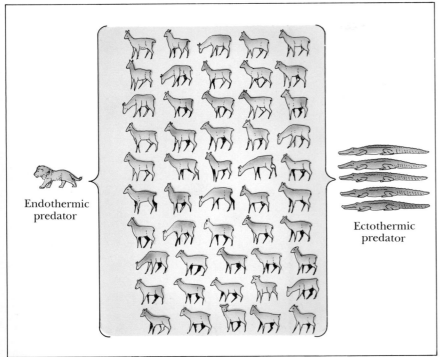

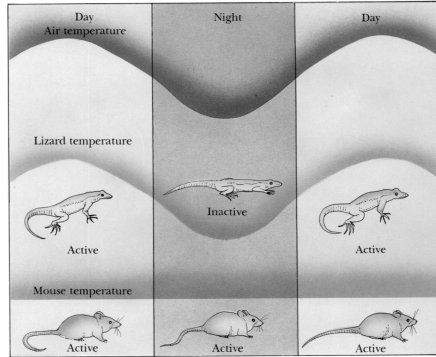

The first dinosaur collectors, in the 1820s and 1830s, thought of them as giant lizards, and thus hefty ectotherms. In 1841, the brilliant English anatomist Richard Owen (later Sir Richard) performed two remarkable feats. Firstly, he published the name "dinosaur" for the first time, as a label to unite the five or six species that had been discovered thus far. Secondly, he argued that the dinosaurs were advanced animals, more comparable with elephants and rhinoceroses, in terms of physiology, than with lizards.

The "mammalian" model of dinosaurian physiology was supported in 1870 by Thomas Huxley, another eminent English palaeontologist, when he pointed out the close resemblances between dinosaurs and birds. He noted in particular the likeness between the smaller theropods and *Archaeopteryx,* the oldest known bird, whose fossils were first found in 1861. However, the idea that the dinosaurs might have been endothermic did not hold sway for long. Most palaeontologists of Victorian times, and for much of this century, saw them as sluggish, swamp-dwelling ectotherms that lived life at a slow pace and had low metabolic rates.

This view was challenged strongly in the early 1970s by Dr Robert Bakker, then of Yale University, in a series of articles. He presented several different lines of evidence that all dinosaurs were, in his opinion, highly active and fully endothermic:

Endotherms like mice have constant body temperatures whatever the air temperature (right), while an ectothermic lizard is dependent on air temperature. Endothermic predators need ten times as much food as ectotherms. Put another way, a certain number of wildebeest would feed one lion for a year — or five crocodiles.

Left: The powerful theropod Allosaurus, *on the left, attacks the herbivorous ornithopod* Camptosaurus, *in an action mount in the Los Angeles County Museum. The proportions of predators and prey in dinosaurian faunas may provide some indication of the thermoregulatory physiology of the predators.*

1. Dinosaurs stood on erect limbs and they show signs of being capable of running at high speeds.

2. The large sauropods must have had advanced hearts, of considerable size, to pump blood up to their heads.

3. Many theropods show adaptations for great agility and so could have had high metabolic rates.

4. Dinosaur fossils have been found within the Cretaceous Arctic Circle, and they must therefore have been able to withstand freezing climates.

5. Dinosaur communities show endothermic predator-prey ratios. This is based on the finding that modern mammal carnivores need ten times more food than ectotherms of the same body weight (see above), and hence the ratio of predators to prey should be close to 1:100 for endotherms, and 10:100 for ectotherms.

6. Dinosaurian bone shows evidence of fast growth and remodelling, as in modern mammalian bone.

7. Certain theropods had largish bird-sized brains rather than relatively small reptile-like brains.

8. Dinosaur skulls lack the pineal opening on top, which is the opening for the "third eye" of many lizards, used in behavioural temperature control by these ectotherms.

9. Birds, which are endotherms, arose from small theropod dinosaurs, and hence dinosaurs were probably endotherms too.

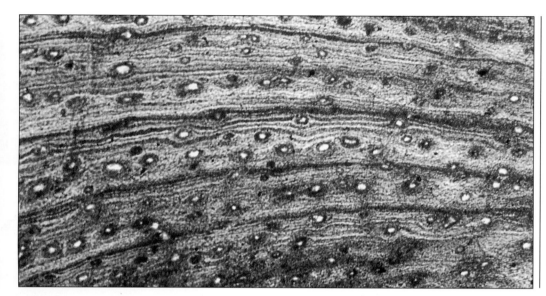

Bakker's suggestions led to a great deal of controversy through the 1970s, which still continues today. His critics noted that most of his arguments were inconclusive (1-9), some were based on too many suppositions to be testable (2, 5, 7, 8), and others were based on mistaken links between anatomy and physiology (1, 6, 7). For example, many ectotherms can move very fast indeed (including plenty of lizards); they cannot sustain these high speeds, however. But we cannot test whether dinosaurs were burst-runners or sustained-runners (1). Also, there is no evidence for extensive glaciation in the Mesozoic, and so temperatures within the Arctic Circle at that time were not so low as they are today (4). And the special "mammalian" features of dinosaurian bone, such as the internal canal pattern, only indicate fast growth and large body size, not endothermy. These features are seen in large ectotherms today, like turtles, while small birds and mammals have supposedly

Microscopic sections of dinosaur bone give evidence of their thermoregulatory (body temperature) physiology. Dinosaurs have the typical zonal bone with growth rings (above), as seen in modern ectotherms that show spurts of growth in summer when food is abundant. However, dinosaurs also have fibro-lamellar bone (right), which indicates fast growth, as seen in larger modern endotherms such as cattle and ostriches.

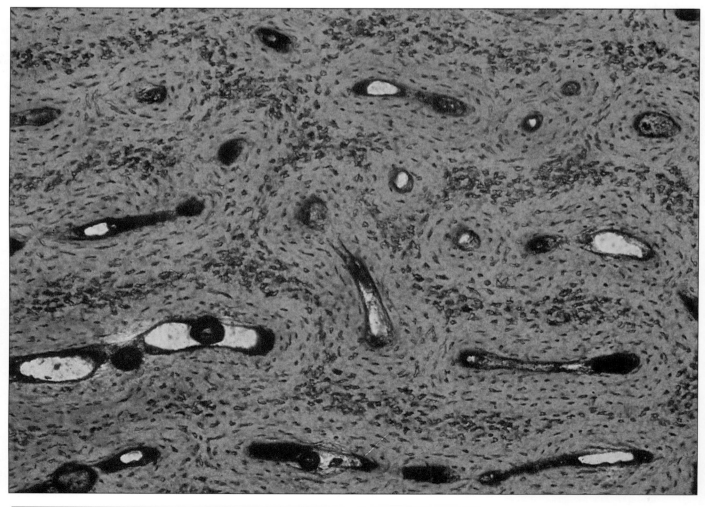

PROTOCERATOPS

The early horned dinosaur Protoceratops *from Mongolia. Numerous skeletons of this ceratopsian were collected by an expedition sent from the American Museum of Natural History to central Asia in the 1920s. Many of the skeletons were associated with nests, eggs and young.* Protoceratops *laid some 20 to 30 sausage-shaped eggs in two or three concentric circles, in a nest hollowed out in the sand.*

"ectothermic" bone, simply because they are small (6).

The arguments today focus on the questions of predator-prey ratios (5), bone structure (6) and energy budgets — the balance of food intake, food quality, and metabolic rate. Bakker still adamantly maintains his views, whereas most other dinosaur palaeontologists admit a compromise position. In this the small advanced theropods had bird-like endothermy, whereas all other dinosaurs (the large and very large ones) had a special thermoregulatory mechanism termed inertial homeothermy or mass homeothermy. This is based on the fact that the fluctuating body temperature of a poikilotherm shows a lag period when compared to fluctuations in air temperature, and the length of the lag depends on body mass. The larger the ectotherm, the more inertia is stored in the body, which slows the rate of cooling at night and slows the rate of warming by day. It has been calculated that most dinosaurs would show fluctuations of only 1-2°C in body temperature, even when air temperatures ranged over 20°C from day to night.

Did dinosaurs care for their young?

Until recently, it was thought that only birds and mammals showed true parental care, and that reptiles typically laid their eggs and then abandoned them to their fate. However, field observations of crocodiles in the 1970s showed that they helped their young to hatch and carried them to the water. It then came as no surprise to scientists studying the subject when, in the 1980s, evidence was unearthed of parental care in dinosaurs.

Dinosaur eggs have been known for a long time, especially from productive deposits in southern France and Mongolia, and more recently from India and the midwest of North America. The famous American Museum expeditions to Mongolia in the 1920s discovered complete fossilized *Protoceratops* nests. Some of these contained several concentric rings of up to 18 eggs, and many were associated with skeletons of adults, juveniles and hatchlings. The French eggs were laid by the sauropod *Hypselosaurus*. These are larger than the *Protoceratops* eggs, and the maximum number in a nest seems to be 12 or 13. Eggs laid by very big dinosaurs were quite small in proportion — rarely more than 30 centimetres long — because of mechanical limitations. The larger an egg the thicker its shell must be, in order to prevent collapse. But beyond a certain thickness, the embryo inside could no longer respire, since oxygen passes through an eggshell to the developing young within. Also, the young would be unable to break out of such a thick shell when the time came.

An important series of excavations by Dr Jack Horner in Montana have demonstrated some important aspects of dinosaurian "child care". He has found nests of hadrosaurs, hypsilophodontid ornithopods and sauropods around the aptly-named "Egg Mountain". The hadrosaur eggs are often positioned in great rounded nests on the ground, and the nests occur in colonies, which suggests communal nesting. Horner found that these dinosaurs returned to the same site to lay their eggs year after year. The nests are low mounds which the female hadrosaur dug out with her hind feet. She laid 24 or so ellipsoidal eggs in concentric rings, covered them with sand, and apparently tended the nest until the young hatched. This is suggested by skeletons of adult and juvenile hadrosaurs, of the genus *Maiasaura*, found all around the nests. The association of nests, hatchlings, juveniles and adults strongly indicates some kind of parental care in which the hatchlings may have been offered food for their first days out of the shell. The presence of adults would also have deterred predators.

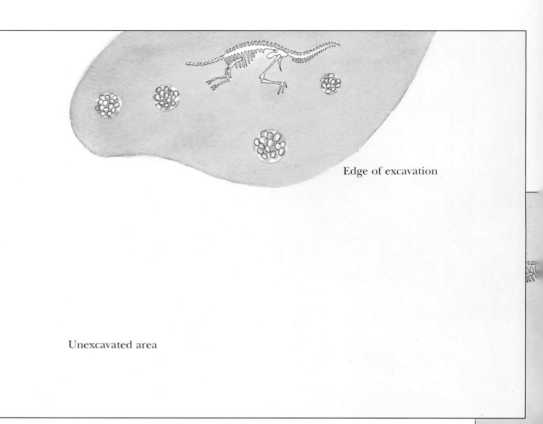

Edge of excavation

Unexcavated area

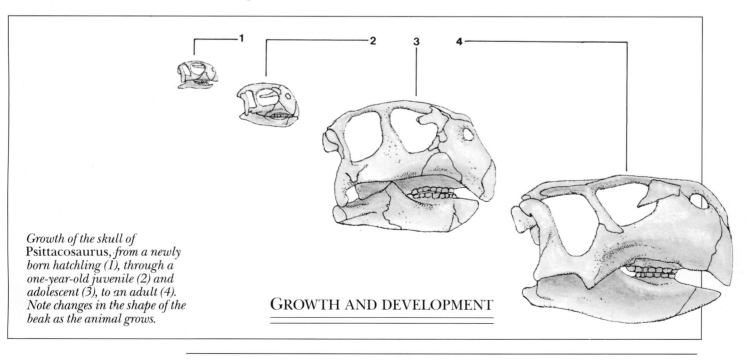

Growth of the skull of Psittacosaurus, *from a newly born hatchling (1), through a one-year-old juvenile (2) and adolescent (3), to an adult (4). Note changes in the shape of the beak as the animal grows.*

GROWTH AND DEVELOPMENT

Left: The excavation levels of "Egg Mountain", Montana. The first level produced a hypsilophodontid skeleton and four nests.

Below: Several metres below, six dinosaur skeletons and four nests were found, as well as a lizard skeleton (top left) and several odd dinosaur eggs scattered throughout.

The iguanodontid **Probactrosaurus** *from Mongolia, displayed in a life-like scene with a mother tending her nest of eggs (right).*

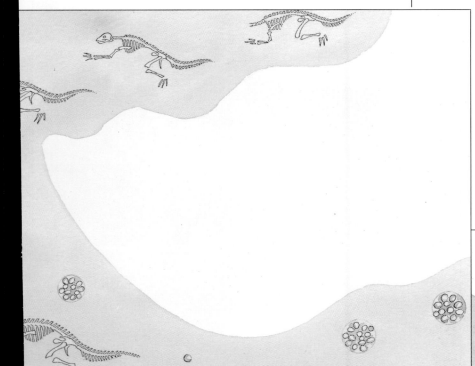

Right: Several more metres down, three hypsilophodontid skeletons and three nests were found. The excavation shows that the dinosaurs returned to the same place year after year to make their nests.

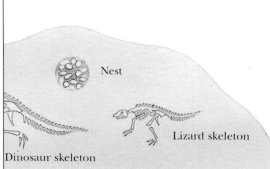

"Odd" dinosaur eggs

Nest

Dinosaur skeleton

Lizard skeleton

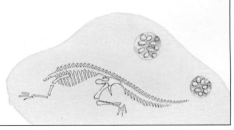

Why were dinosaurs so large?

Although there were some chicken-sized dinosaurs in existence, on average they were an order of magnitude larger than mammals. In other words, a graph of the range of typical dinosaur sizes would be like a similar graph for mammals, but multiplied by ten. Why did dinosaurs live on such a scale, and how did they cope?

The answer to the "why" question may simply be that dinosaurs were large because nothing else was. Mammals have not achieved such giant sizes as the great sauropods simply because of the vast food requirements of a 30-metre-long endotherm. It is not correct to assume that a *Brontosaurus*-sized mammal would have to eat ten times as much as an ectothermic *Brontosaurus*, because both would gain the same advantages of inertial homeothermy. However, being ectothermic may have freed the sauropods from this type of energy-gathering constraint against giant size, that may be holding back the elephants.

What problems did the huge dinosaurs face because of their size? The most serious must have been the biomechanical stresses of vast bulk. Every bone of a vertebrate skeleton, and every muscle, is constructed to a certain size and strength, which depends on the stresses it normally undergoes. For instance the diameter of an animal's leg is directly proportional to its body weight, for the simple

Diplodocus, the longest completely known dinosaur, reaches 27 metres (right). The immensely long neck and tail created enormous biomechanical challenges for this sauropod: powerful muscles were needed to lift the head up and down, and the backbone had to have extra strength to prevent the massive body from collapsing.

When dinosaur skeletons were first mounted in museums in the 19th century, their great size caused much wonderment. Stegosaurus, seen in this 1891 picture, was a typical example (below).

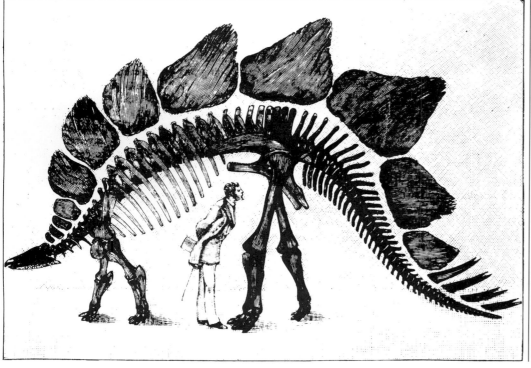

reason that weight-supporting pillars have to be scaled correctly. There is a built-in safety factor, as in the design of a building, so that an animal's legs can withstand unusual, but not excessive, stresses. Human legs could support two or three times the body's normal weight and they can deal with the impact of a long jump. They could not cope if they had to support the mass of an elephant or if you jumped down more than about five metres.

Biological structures have built-in safety factors of these kinds but they are not excessive, because of the "cost" of building and maintaining unnecessarily safe structures. A balance is struck between everyday needs and possible unusual demands on a structure, and the costs of construction and maintenance, in the same way that a civil engineer calculates the minimum materials required for a building to be safe.

The problems for the big dinosaurs depended on the area : volume relationship mentioned previously. The diameter of a leg (a square measure) is proportional to the weight of the animal (a cubic measure). Hence, as the weight increases, the leg diameter has to increase in proportion to volume (not to body surface area). The limbs of an elephant are out of scale with those of a gazelle, if their bodies are drawn to the same size; the gazelle has narrow stick-like legs while the elephant has massive pillars. The area : volume effect meant that the legs of the large sauropods were even more massive, relatively, than those of an elephant. Calculations show that, at a body weight of much more than 100 tonnes, a four-legged animal would have legs so like tree trunks it could barely walk. Larger still and it would be immobile, and in any case would probably disappear into the ground under its own weight!

There has been much debate over the estimated weights of dinosaurs, and which was heaviest. Weights are calculated from accurate scale models. The exact volume of a model is obtained by the amount of water it displaces from a measuring cylinder, and the volume is converted to weight by a factor representing the volume : weight ratio of crocodile flesh. This is then scaled up to the size of the dinosaur in life. However, estimates vary greatly. One of the contenders for largest dinosaur, *Brachiosaurus*, has had its weight estimated at anywhere from 20 to 78 tonnes — on the basis of the same skeletons! Its relative, *Ultrasaurus*, might have been even heavier (weights in the range 100-140 tonnes have been quoted), but the remains are far too incomplete to tell. Many other dinosaurs seem to have exceeded the 50-tonne mark, according to a 1988 review by Dr Greg Paul of Colorado. These include the diplodocid *Supersaurus*, the titanosaur *Antarctosaurus*, various unnamed

A prosauropod footprint and handprint from the Early Jurassic Kayenta Formation of Arizona (above). The footprint was made in firm mud. It shows what kind of dinosaur made the track, and also other information that can be used in calculating speeds.

specimens based on single huge bones and even some based on massive fossilized trackways.

The equations that lead to the calculation of a maximum size limit are made more complex by adding the effects of locomotion. Animals use their legs for walking and running, and these activities put the limbs under multiplied stresses. If your body weight exerts a force x through each foot when you are standing still, that force can increase to 10x when you are running because of the impact of each footfall. The stress on the leg bones is further increased by the fact that when the impact occurs, the limb is not at right angles to the ground. Hence the force of impact is not transmitted parallel to the long axis of each leg bone, but at an angle to that axis, so producing an angled stress that tends to fracture the bone. These factors limited the large sauropods to relatively slow walking. At a gallop, *Brontosaurus* would have broken his legs!

Who are the dinosaurs' closest living relatives?

Dinosaurs have always been regarded as reptiles, and their closest living relatives were assumed to be the crocodilians. It is easy to see why. After all, a scaly crocodile, with its great

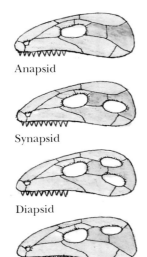

Anapsid

Synapsid

Diapsid

Euryapsid

jaws and long teeth, seems primeval enough to be a living dinosaur. Closer analysis of their anatomy shows that the crocodilians are archosaurs ("ruling reptiles") like the dinosaurs and pterosaurs: they have the "skull windows" known as the antorbital fenestra (at least the fossil forms do) and mandibular fenestra, and the fourth trochanter on the femur.

Correctly speaking, however, the closest living relatives of the dinosaurs are birds. This has been implied for many years, but not stated so clearly until fairly recent times. Huxley, in his 1870 paper, was quite clear that *Archaeopteryx* was simply a feathered dinosaur, and that birds as a group arose from the small theropods. However, the clarity of this view was muddied throughout much of the present century by an excess of hypotheses concerning the fossil facts, and also by the search for elusive "ancestors" of the birds very far back in time. There was a feeling that *Archaeopteryx,* in the Late Jurassic some 150 million years ago, was far too bird-like to have arisen from theropods that lived about the same time; the ancestry of birds should be sought some 70 million years earlier, in the Late Triassic. Hence, the view gained ground that the birds arose directly from thecodon-

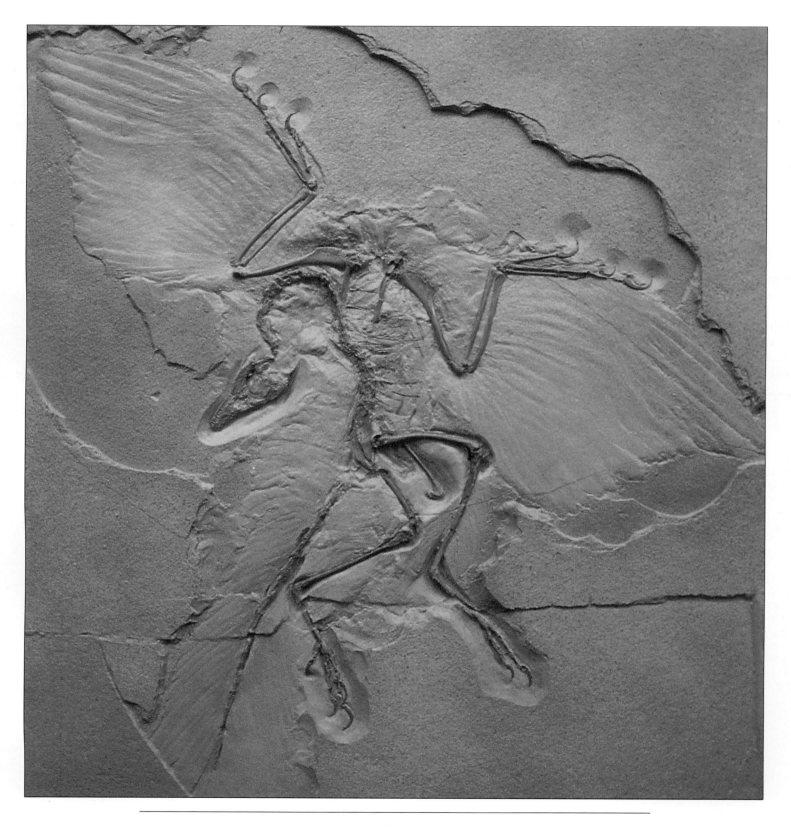

tians, and their long intervening history was totally devoid of fossils. Of course, several supposed Late Triassic and Early Jurassic "birds" have been reported, but none has yet turned out to be a true bird.

In the 1970s some palaeontologists, particularly Prof. John Ostrom of Yale University, challenged the thecodontian/bird model. Ostrom reiterated a great deal of Huxley's arguments a century before, and showed that in every respect the skeletons of *Archaeopteryx* and later birds matched the skeletons of theropods such as *Deinonychus*. The resemblances he noted are so striking that it seems incredible that his ideas were resisted — and they still are by some palaeontologists. The resistance is especially strange in view of the fact that there is no evidence in favour of alternative hypotheses.

Ostrom's arguments were taken up by various cladistic analysts (see page 16), who found them compelling. The birds fit neatly at the end of a sequence of ever more bird-like theropods, starting with *Coelophysis* at the bottom and leading up through the tyrannosaurs, ornithomimids, coelurids, and others, to the dromaeosaurids, troodontids and finally the birds themselves. Indeed, many typically

Archaeopteryx, the oldest known fossil bird (left). This is the "Berlin" specimen, found in 1877, showing excellent preservation of its feathers.

"avian" characters were already present in various theropods. Some palaeontologists even argue that feathers, the key bird synapomorphy, were present in some or all of the theropod dinosaurs. There is, as yet, no direct evidence for this intriguing suggestion.

Running and leaping dinosaurs

Until recently, many palaeontologists had mental images of dinosaurian locomotion that were probably not dissimilar from the lumbering "freeze-frame" models seen in the early monster movies. The giant dinosaurs blundered along in slow motion, stepping on trees and other animals which were crushed beneath their feet in their mindless, tank-like progression. Ideas have changed, now that it is possible to calculate exactly how fast dinosaurs could run.

The main evidence comes from footprints (see page 42) which give two pieces of useful information. First, the prints generally show which dinosaur made the tracks by their size, the number of toes and the overall shape of each print. In many cases, it is possible to see the impressions of the joints in the fingers and toes, and to match these with skeletons excavated from rocks of the same age nearby.

COMPARATIVE BONE STRUCTURES

The arms (left) and legs (right) of birds and theropod dinosaurs are very similar. The arm of Deinonychus *(1) has the three long narrow fingers seen in* Archaeopteryx *(2), which are fused and reduced in* Columba, *the modern pigeon (3). The legs show even less change. The dinosaur* Compsognathus *(4) already has the three-toed foot of* Archaeopteryx *(5) and* Columba *(6). The main changes are fusion of the tibia and fibula (shin bones), and fusion of the tarsals and metatarsals (ankle and foot bones) in modern birds.*

Second, the spacing of the footprints in a fossilized trackway gives the precise stride length. In 1976 Prof R McNeill Alexander, of Leeds University, England, established a mathematical relationship between the stride length and the limb length of all vertebrates, which gave their speed of locomotion. He discovered that this relationship applied to animals as diverse as horses, humans, dogs, elephants and ostriches.

In calculating the speeds of dinosaurs, McNeill Alexander could read the stride length directly from fossilized trackways, and he could calculate the limb length with a fair degree of confidence from a matching skeleton. The speeds he obtained ranged from 4 to 6 kilometres per hour for giant sauropods such as *Apatosaurus*, and 6 to 8.5 kilometres per hour for theropods such as *Megalosaurus*. Since 1976, palaeontologists have applied this formula to a great number of dinosaur trackways, and they found that most larger dinosaurs tended to move at such stately speeds, in most cases little faster than human walking.

However, some trackways did yield faster speeds. Certain medium-sized theropod tracks gave speeds of up to 16.5 kilometres per hour, close to the fastest running speed of a human being. Even greater speeds, at up to 42 kilometres per hour, were calculated for smaller carnivores; while the 45 to 50 kilometres per hour for tyrannosaurs was closer to that of a galloping racehorse.

The question of dinosaurian speed has great implications for their physiology, and there have been acrimonious disputes over the methods of calculation and even the validity of using the preserved trackways in the first place. The proponents of endothermy in dinosaurs (see page 112) argue that even large forms were fleet of foot and capable of galloping. These palaeobiologists are convinced that there is little point in calculating dinosaur speeds from trackways, since these are unlikely to give maximum rates. After all, they argue, a large dinosaur was unlikely to be moving at top speed as it ploughed through the mud in which it left its tracks. When it galloped over the dusty plains at full tilt, no prints were left to be preserved.

The proponents of ectothermy in dinosaurs argue that trackways are least well preserved in swamps and bogs: the mud soon runs back into the prints, and after a few minutes nothing can be seen. They contend that the clearest footprints are formed in firm sand, as can be demonstrated on the beach today, and so high running speeds would be possible. They note the consistency of all the calculations in positing human walking speeds for the largest dinosaurs, and fast speeds only for smaller theropods.

The three-toed footprint of Megalosaurus *(above) and two five-toed footprints of an amphibian (right), which lived at about the time of the origin of the dinosaurs.*

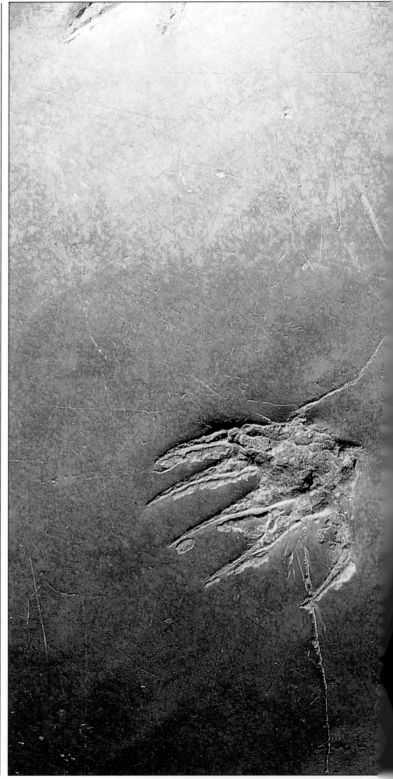

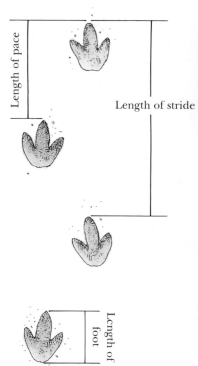

Length of pace

Length of stride

Length of foot

A dinosaur trackway offers a great deal of information for biomechanical analysis (above). The footprint size and shape identify the track maker, while the stride length (or the pace length) indicates the speed of movement.

There is also the question of limb structure. Most experts in biomechanics, the study of plants and animals as engineering constructions, now argue that the really large sauropods were under several material constraints because of their huge size. The limb bones were strong enough for walking, and even fast walking, but not for galloping, since the stresses on bone rise rapidly as the speed of locomotion increases. Modern elephants and rhinoceroses can gallop, but they seem to be at the upper size limit for this fast mode of moving. Detailed analyses of dinosaur legs suggest that the stegosaurs, ceratopsians and ankylosaurs were probably capable of galloping at elephant-like speeds, too. The smaller two-legged theropods, free of such mechanical size constraints, could pick up considerable speeds if necessary to escape predation or catch fast-moving food. But the notion of a seven-tonne *Tyrannosaurus* hurtling along at 50 kilometres per hour is still so appalling that most biologists would find it hard to accept!

Why did the dinosaurs die out?

The extinction of the dinosaurs is the key question that everyone asks. Remarkably the answer is still not known, even though so many scientists have tried to tackle it. At present, some 500 or more palaeontologists, geologists, geochemists and astrophysicists are working on the problem. Hundreds of research papers are published each year on the subject, and dozens of meetings are held, but we seem no nearer the truth than we were ten years ago. We still cannot say with certainty whether the dinosaurs took ten million years or one minute to die out, nor whether they died out simultaneously in all parts of the world. This may seem a poor state of affairs.

Broad measures of dinosaurian diversity show that during the latter half of their history, at any one time some 20 or 30 families were in existence, and the global species diversity (as far as we know) was 50-100. These figures are probably far from the truth, because of the incompleteness of the fossil record and the problems of dating rocks accurately; but it is likely that they are equally inaccurate for each span of time. Thus, they can give a qualitative measure of the situation, if not a quantitative one.

In 1984, Dr Dale Russell of the National Museum of Natural Sciences in Ottawa, Canada, plotted overall figures of the global diversity of dinosaurs through time, in an attempt to show that disappearance of the dinosaurs was indeed sudden. Their diversity held up right to the end, with no sign of the drop-off one would expect from a more gradual disappearance. On the other hand, Dr Robert

The speeds of modern animals, such as these wolves (above), may be recorded precisely. It is less easy to assess whether carnivorous dinosaurs could run as fast, but their footprints give strong evidence that small theropods could.

Two small dromaeosaurs attack a much larger hadrosaur (right). These fast-moving theropods probably hunted in packs and may have chased a larger herbivore for some distance until it weakened.

Sloan of the University of Minnesota, Minneapolis, and his colleagues published a paper in 1986 that suggested the opposite. Their study was based on decades of collecting dinosaur and mammal bones in the Hell Creek Formation of Montana. Their graphs, based on hundreds of bones and a finer quality of dating, seemed to show a long-term decline of the dinosaurs over eight million years or so, and a matching radiation of the mammals. A 1987 study by Dr Bob Sullivan of the Los Angeles County Museum, California, seemed to bear this out on a global scale. He found that dinosaurian diversity declined from 16 families to nine in the last 10 million years of the Cretaceous. The "last" dinosaurs amounted to 12 species, known from only a few dozen specimens worldwide. His analysis has been criticized, however, because of problems in correlating dinosaur-bearing rocks worldwide (they just cannot be dated as precisely as Sullivan suggested) and problems in establishing the true numbers of species present.

These debates concern the *pattern* of extinction, and the contrasting views have been characterized in the question: did the dinosaurs disappear with a bang (the Russell view) or a whimper (the Sloan-Sullivan view)? If the pattern

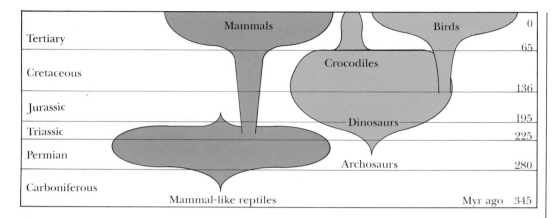

cannot be established in the first place, how on earth can scientists even begin to establish the *process* that produced the pattern? Each postulated pattern is supported by roughly equal numbers of scientists, whose proposals are often called the "gradualist" (whimper) and "catastrophist" (bang) explanations.

The "gradualist" model

The main thrust of the gradualist model is that climates were changing in the long term, possibly as a result of varying sea levels, and the dinosaurs disappeared as a result of loss of suitable habitats. This is accepted in one form or another by many palaeontologists and geologists. The main evidence is palaeontological; detailed studies in certain sedimentary basins seem to show a long-term decline of the dinosaurs, as well as of many other groups that disappeared at the same time (pterosaurs and some crocodilians, birds and mammals on land, and plesiosaurs, ichthyosaurs, mosasaurs, ammonites and belemnites in the sea). Further support comes from the evidence that sea levels rose during the end of the Cretaceous and flooded coastal regions, and climates seem to have become temperate in many dinosaur habitats. Leigh Van Valen, of Chicago University and Robert Sloan have noted how the lush subtropical vegetation of dinosaur times seemed to give way to temperate conifer forests over a time span of 5-10 million years. It is believed that this changeover parallels exactly the decline of the dinosaurs and the rise of the mammals.

The "castastrophist" scenario

The opposing catastrophist view has gained much more publicity recently, and the support of geochemists and astrophysicists in particular. For years, geologists had suggested that the dinosaurs might have been killed off by meteorite strikes, solar flares or supernovas (exploding

The age of the dinosaurs was only one stage in the sequence of life. The land was dominated in the Late Carboniferous, Permian and much of the Triassic by the mammal-like reptiles (above). They gave rise to the mammals, but in the meantime the dinosaurs took over in the Late Triassic, Jurassic and Cretaceous. After the demise of the dinosaurs, the mammals multiplied and spread from 66 million years ago.

Did the dinosaurs succumb to global cooling? An imaginative restoration of a pair of Tyrannosaurus rex being overwhelmed by icy weather that followed from a major extraterrestrial impact or volcanic activity (right). This "global winter" is analogous to the "nuclear winter" predicted to follow a nuclear war.

stars), but they were generally regarded as idle speculators by the palaeontologists. In 1980, however, Luis Alvarez (a Nobel Prize-winning physicist from Berkeley, California) and his associates, published a seminal report that set the catastrophist bandwaggon rolling. They reported increased levels of the rare metal iridium (related to platinum) in a thin clay layer dated at the Cretaceous-Tertiary boundary, from a site at Gubbio, in Italy. On the basis of this observation, they proposed that the Earth had been struck by an asteroid some ten kilometres in diameter; the force of the impact sent clouds of dust into the upper atmosphere, which blacked out the sun, and led to worldwide catastrophic extinctions.

Many geologists poured scorn on this notion initially, since they thought an unnecessarily dramatic theory had been cooked up on the basis of very limited evidence. However, the enhanced iridium clay, or "iridium spike", was found at more than 50 localities worldwide in the following four years, in sediments that had been deposited under the sea, in lakes and in rivers. What did it mean?

Iridium is not a natural constituent of the Earth's crust, but arrives in meteorites and other debris from space. It occurs naturally only in the core of the Earth, and it may be brought up to the crust and the surface by certain unusual kinds of volcanoes. This is why Alvarez and his team immediately postulated an extraterrestrial source for the iridium they had identified — and a very large source, to produce the enhanced levels at the Cretaceous/Tertiary (K/T) boundary. On the basis of a single location, they predicted the occurrence of the iridium spike at every site where the K/T boundary was studied; their prediction was amply borne out in the following years. This won a large number of scientists to their cause.

There is now a variety of other evidence in favour of the catastrophist model of K/T extinction. Certain fossil groups, especially marine plankton, show very sudden extinctions at the boundary. There were also major short-term perturbations of land plants. Immediately above the iridium spike in many geological rock sections is a "fern spike". This is interpreted to show the disappearance of the normal angiosperm plants (flowers and trees), followed by an initial spread of ferns but then the recovery of angiosperms some years later. This is exactly what happens after major volcanic eruptions, and the K/T fern spike is said to demonstrate a global blanket of sterile dust following the asteroid impact, and then the gradual germination of buried spores and seeds.

Additional evidence for impact includes the occurrence of glassy spherules (tiny "marbles") in association with the

iridium-rich clays. These supposedly result from the melting of the impact materials. A similar strand of evidence is grains of "shocked quartz". These show two or more sets of parallel lines running across the platy grains when examined under the microscope, and such strain features can apparently be produced only by impact.

The gradualist geologists and palaeontologists argue that many of these features could be produced by large-scale volcanic eruptions. They point to great thicknesses of lava of about the right age in the Deccan traps of India as a possible source of global dust clouds, iridium, glassy spherules and shocked quartz.

The main weakness of the impact scenario is that it does not fit the biological facts, in several ways. Firstly, life was not wiped out globally and instantaneously, so far as we can tell. In fact, most groups of plants and animals passed through the K/T boundary totally unaffected. Secondly, most of the groups that died out did so in a gradual, long-term way. The beginnings of the K/T extinctions can be traced back as far as 30 million years previously for some marine groups, even if the evidence for a decline of dinosaurs is still equivocal. Thirdly, the "killing models" following the impact are not biologically acceptable and do not fit the evidence. It has been suggested that the asteroid raised a vast dust cloud to block out the sun; or it caused overheating of the Earth when it entered the atmosphere;

The extraterrestrial catastrophe model for the extinction of the dinosaurs (below). A massive asteroid, or a shower of comets, hurtles through the atmosphere and hits the Earth, either in the sea or in parts of central North America. The impact is so great that millions of tonnes of rock and dust are sent into the atmosphere, forming a vast dust cloud that sweeps all round the globe. The Sun is blocked out for many months, leading to intense cold, a temporary end to plant growth, and widespread extinction of plants and animals.

or the explosion on impact released poisonous arsenic or osmium into the atmosphere; or the asteroid landed in the sea and sent huge tidal waves (tsunamis) hurtling round the world, destroying all lowland terrestrial life with its 30-metre-high wave fronts. Some sediments near the K/T boundary do show evidence for tsunamis, but it seems incredible that these would have wiped out the dinosaurs and pterosaurs, yet left the lizards, turtles, crocodiles and most mammals unaffected.

Today's consensus?

The current consensus, if there is any consensus at all, is that there was an impact, of an asteroid or a shower of comets, at the K/T boundary — but this was not the sole cause of extinction. There is no question that the belemnites and ichthyosaurs had already gone before the K/T boundary, and that most other groups were in long-term decline. However, it seems likely that the final extinctions coincided with the impact, although that cannot yet be established on a global scale.

The extinctions saga goes far beyond the K/T event, since there were many other extinctions both before and after it. These other events have attracted less attention than the K/T one, because they do not involve the disappearance of the dinosaurs, and also the actual boundary rocks are not so widely available for study.

10km asteroid

Asteroid makes impact with Earth

These various events have been tied together by a new debate on the periodicity of extinctions: do they follow a regular cyclical pattern, and is their occurrence predictable? If so — and many accept the periodicity of extinctions now — what causes the periodicity? The extraterrestrial model has been expanded to form an explanation. Regular showers of comets hit the Earth every 26 million years; and the regular intervals between showers is produced by a major astronomical phenomenon. This is possibly a twin star to our sun, called Nemesis, which follows an eccentric orbit that brings it close to the solar system every 26 million years; possibly it concerns tilting of the whole galactic plane; or even an unseen "planet X" beyond Pluto, which swings in to disturb the edge of the solar system every 26 million years. Astrophysicists now hold conferences on these models, and it all started with the dinosaurs!

If this is not enough, the modelling of asteroid impact effects has had an enormous impact during the last decade. The computer models showed that the great dust cloud which rose into the air at the time of the K/T boundary, blacked out the sun and cut off the infra-red rays that warm the surface of the Earth. The atmospheric modellers calculated that the dust cloud lowered global surface temperatures by 20°C or more, to produce a "global winter" that killed off the warmth-loving dinosaurs (but what about the crocodiles and lizards?) These calculations led directly to

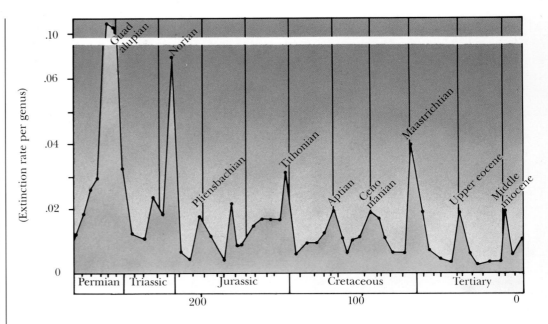

Periodicity of mass extinctions, based on a new database of marine organisms (above). Peaks of extinction follow a rough cycle every 26 million years, but the timing is poor in places.

the realization that a major nuclear war today would have exactly the same effect: the famous "Nuclear Winter". Again, this major field of scientific research started about 1982 — with the dinosaurs!

Rocks and dust sent into the upper atmosphere by the force of the impact

Dust cloud blankets the Earth

The sunlight is blocked out for six months to two years, leading to icy cold and widespread extinction.

DINOSAURS OF THE LATE CRETACEOUS

A colourful scene in the famous dinosaur world of southern Alberta about 70 million years ago. By that time, the continents had begun to drift apart — the Atlantic Ocean had opened — and different dinosaur faunas are found in different parts of the world. The main change in the landscape is the appearance of flowering plants — early relatives of magnolias and roses — which radiated in the last 60-70 million years of the Cretaceous.

The commonest dinosaurs were the duckbilled hadrosaurs, which appeared with all shapes and sizes of cranial crests, while the horned ceratopsians were also common. Carnivores included the advanced lightweight troodontids, which fed on frogs, lizards, mammals, birds and pterosaurs, if they could catch them. The largest carnivorous dinosaur, *Tyrannosaurus* (not shown), fed on the hadrosaurs.

How the world looked in this period

The rare carnivorous troodontid, Saurornithoides *(1), was a tiny animal compared with the ceratopsian* Triceratops *(2), the hadrosaurs* Edmontosaurus *(3),* Parasaurolophus *(4), and* Corythosaurus *(5), which fed in great numbers on low bushes and trees and considerably exceeded human size.*

1 2 3 4 5

134

DINOSAUR NAMES

To the uninitiated the jaw-cracking names of dinosaurs can be difficult to pronounce. Below is a guide to help, and a note on what each name means. Often these impenetrable Greek or Latin tags stand for highly descriptive labels which succinctly summarize each dinosaur's idiosyncrasies or appearance — for example, *Ornitholestes* means "bird robber" and *Dromæosaurus* "running reptile".

The scientists who named the dinosaurs are supplied below, and the dates when papers describing the new finds were first published. In most cases the palaeontologists who named the beasts were the same people who dug them up or paid to dig them up.

Allosaurus
AL-oh-SAW-rus
Different reptile
O.C. March 1877

Anchiceratops
AN-ki-SER-a-tops
Close-horned face
B. Brown 1914

Anchisaurus
AN-ki-SAW-rus
Close reptile
O.C. Marsh 1885

Ankylosaurus
ANK-ih-low-SAW-rus
Stiff reptile
B. Brown 1908

Apatosaurus
a-PAT-oh-SAW-rus
Deceptive reptile
O.C. Marsh 1877

Arrhinoceratops
a-RINE-oh-SER-a-tops
No nose-horn face
W. Parks 1925

Barosaurus
BAR-oh-SAW-rus
Heavy reptile
O.C. Marsh 1890

Baryonyx
BAR-ee-ON-ix
Heavy claw
A.J. Charig & A.C. Milner
1986

Brachiosaurus
BRAK-ee-oh-SAW-rus
Arm reptile
E.S. Riggs 1903

Brachyceratops
BRAK-ee-SER-a-tops
Short-horned face
C.W. Gilmore 1914

Brontosaurus
BRON-toe-SAW-rus
Thunder reptile
O.C. Marsh 1879

Camarasaurus
KAM-a-ra-SAW-rus
Chambered reptile
E.D. Cope 1877

Camptosaurus
KAMP-toe-SAW-rus
Flexible reptile
O.C. Marsh 1885

Centrosaurus
SEN-troe-SAW-rus
Sharp point reptile
L.M. Lambe 1904

Ceratosaurus
SER-a-toe-SAW-rus
Horned reptile
O.C. Marsh 1884

Cetiosaurus
SEET-ee-oh-SAW-rus
Whale reptile
R. Owen 1841

Chasmosaurus
KAZ-moe-SAW-rus
Gape reptile
L.M. Lambe 1914

Coelophysis
SEEL-oh-FY-sis
Hollow form
E.D. Cope 1889

Compsognathus
komp-SOG-nath-us
Pretty jaw
J.A. Wagner 1859

Corythosaurus
KOR-ih-tho-SAW-rus
Helmeted reptile
B. Brown 1914

Datousaurus
DAH-toe-SAW-rus
Big-headed reptile
Dong Z. & Tang Z, 1984

Deinonychus
dyne-ON-ik-us
Terrible claw
J.H. Ostrom 1969

Dicraeosaurus
dye-CREE-oh-SAW-rus
Forked reptile
W. Janensch 1929

Diplodocus
dip-LOD-oh-kus
Double beam
O.C. Marsh 1878

Dromaeosaurus
DROME-ee-oh-SAW-rus
Running reptile
W.D. Matthew & B. Brown
1922

Dryosaurus
DRY-oh-SAW-rus
Oak reptile
O.C. Marsh 1894

Edmontosaurus
ed-MONT-oh-SAW-rus
Edmonton reptile
L.M. Lambe 1917

Elaphrosaurus
ee-LAF-roe-SAW-rus
Lightweight reptile
W. Janensch 1920

Euoplocephalus
yoo-OP-low-KEF-al-us
True plated head
L.M. Lambe 1910

Gasosaurus
GAS-oh-SAW-rus
Gas reptile
Dong Z. & Tang Z. 1985

Halticosaurus
HAL-tik-oh-SAW-rus
Springing reptile
F. von Huene 1908

Heterodontosaurus
HET-er-oh-DONT-oh-SAW-rus
Different-tooth reptile
A.W. Crompton & A.J. Charig 1962

Hypselosaurus
HIP-sel-oh-SAW-rus
High reptile
P. Matheron 1869

Hypsilophodon
hip-sih-LOFF-oh-don
High-ridged tooth
T.H. Huxley 1870

Iguanodon
ig-WA-no-don
Iguana tooth
G.A. Mantell 1825

Kentrosaurus
KEN-tro-SAW-rus
Thorn reptile
E. Hennig 1915

Lambeosaurus
LAM-bee-oh-SAW-rus
Lambe's reptile
W. Parks 1923

Leptoceratops
LEP-toe-SER-a-tops
Slim-horned face
B. Brown 1914

Lufengosaurus
loo-FUNG-oh-SAW-rus
Lufeng reptile
C.C. Young 1941

Maiasaura
MY-a-SAW-ra
Good-mother reptile
J.R. Horner & R. Makela 1979

Mamenchisaurus
ma-MUN-chee-SAW-rus
Mamenchi reptile
C.C. Young 1954

Megalosaurus
MEG-a-low-SAW-rus
Great reptile
W. Buckland 1824

Monoclonius
MON-oh-KLONE-ee-us
Single horn
E.D. Cope 1876

Ornitholestes
or-NITH-oh-LESS-teez
Bird robber
H.F. Osborn 1903

Ouranosaurus
oo-RAN-oh-SAW-rus
Brave reptile
P. Taquet 1976

Oviraptor
OVE-ih-RAP-tor
Egg thief
H.F. Osborn 1924

Parasaurolophus
PAR-a-sawr-OL-oh-fus
Parallel-sided reptile
W. Parks 1923

Pelorosaurus
pel-O-roe-SAW-rus
Huge reptile
G.A. Mantell 1850

Pentaceratops
PEN-ta-SER-a-tops
Five-horned face
H.F. Osborn 1923

Pisanosaurus
pis-AN-oh-SAW-rus
Pisano's reptile
J.F. Bonaparte 1976

Plateosaurus
PLAT-ee-oh-SAW-rus
Flat reptile
H. von Meyer 1837

Probactrosaurus
pro-BAK-trow-SAW-rus
Before the Bactrian reptile
A.K. Rozhdestvensky 1966

Procompsognathus
PRO-komp-SOG-nath-us
Before *Compsognathus*
E. Fraas 1913

Protoceratops
pro-toe-SER-a-tops
First horned-face
W. Granger & W.K. Gregory 1923

Psittacosaurus
SIT-a-ko-SAW-rus
Parrot reptile
H.F. Osborn 1923

Saltasaurus
SALT-a-SAW-rus
Salta reptile
J.F. Bonaparte & J. Powell 1980

Saurolophus
sawr-ROL-oh-fus
Ridged reptile
B. Brown 1912

Saurornithoides
sawr-OR-nith-OI-deez
Bird-like reptile
H.F. Osborn 1924

Scolosaurus
SKOLE-oh-SAW-rus
Thorn reptile
F. Nopsca 1928

Shunosaurus
SHOO-no-SAW-rus
Shu (Sichuan) reptile
Dong Z., Zhow S. & Chang Y. 1983

Stegoceras
steg-OSS-er-as
Horny roof
L.M. Lambe 1902

Struthiomimus
STROOTH-ee-oh-MIME-us
Ostrich mimic
H.F. Osborn 1917

Styracosaurus
sty-RAK-oh-SAW-rus
Spiked reptile
L.M. Lambe 1913

Supersaurus
Soop-er-SAW-rus
Super reptile
J. Jensen 1985

Talarurus
TAL-ah-ROO-rus
Basket tail
E.A. Maleev 1952

Torosaurus
TOR-oh-SAW-rus
Piercing reptile
O.C. Marsh 1891

Triceratops
try-SER-a-tops
Three-horned face
O.C. Marsh 1889

Tsintaosaurus
CHING-dah-oo-SAW-rus
Reptile from Chingtao
C.C. Young 1958

Tuojiangosaurus
TOO-oh-JEE-ang-o-SAW-rus
Tuojiang reptile
Dong Z., Li X., Zhow S. & Chang Y. 1977

Tyrannosaurus
tie-RAN-oh-SAW-rus
Tyrant reptile
H.F. Osborn 1905

Ultrasaurus
ULL-tra-SAW-rus
Ultra reptile
J. Jensen 1985

Xiaosaurus
sheeyow-SAW-rus
Dawn reptile
Dong Z. & Tang Z. 1983

MUSEUMS

This listing gives the names of the main dinosaur museums in the world. The listing is by continent, and a brief note is given of important exhibits in each museum.

The list is not definitive — as new discoveries are being made collections are being added to all the time and, occasionally, touring exhibitions may take up residence.

AFRICA

Bernard Price Institute of Palaeontology, Johannesburg, South Africa. Triassic and Jurassic prosauropods.

Musée National du Niger, Niamey, Niger. The Early Cretaceous sail-backed *Ouranosaurus.*

Museum of Earth Sciences, Rabat, Morocco. Early sauropods *Cetiosaurus* and *Rebbachisaurus.*

National Museum of Zimbabwe, Harare, Zimbabwe. Early Jurassic *Syntarsus* and *Vulcanodon*

South African Museum, Cape Town, South Africa. Triassic and Jurassic prosauropods of all sizes.

ASIA

Beipei Museum, Beipei, China. New mounts of Chinese Jurassic dinosaurs.

Indian Statistical Institute, Calcutta, India. Early sauropod *Barapasaurus.*

Institute of Vertebrate Palaeontology and Palaeoanthropology, Peking, China. Large collection of Chinese Triassic, Jurassic and Cretaceous dinosaurs.

Mongolian Academy of Sciences, Ulan Bator, Mongolia. Late Cretaceous duckbills and ceratopsians.

National Science Museum, Tokyo. Various Japanese fossil reptiles.

AUSTRALIA

Australian Museum, Sydney, New South Wales. Australian fossils and North American casts.

Queensland Museum, Fortitude Valley, Queensland. Early sauropod *Rhoetosaurus* and ornithopod *Muttaburrasaurus.*

EUROPE

Bayerische Staatssammlung fur Geologie und historische Geologie, Munich, West Germany. Tiny theropod *Compsognathus.*

Bernissart Museum, Bernissart, Belgium. Locally-collected *Iguanodon.*

Birmingham Museum, Birmingham, England. Casts of US dinosaurs.

Central Geological and Prospecting Museum, Leningrad, USSR. Asian dinosaurs and casts of others.

British Museum (Natural History), London, England. Casts of large North American dinosaurs; *Baryonyx.*

The Dinosaur Museum, Dorchester, England. English Wealden dinosaurs.

Institut und Museum fur Geologie und Paläontologie, Tübingen, West Germany. *Plateosaurus* and casts of others.

Institut Royal des Sciences Naturelles, Brussels, Belgium. Mount of 20 or so *Iguanodon.*

Institute of Paleobiology, Warsaw, Poland. Large collection of Mongolian dinosaurs.

Leicestershire Museum, Leicester, England. New *Cetiosaurus* skeleton.

Museum of Isle of Wight Geology, Sandown, England. Local early Cretaceous dinosaurs.

NORTH AMERICA

Museum National d'Histoire Naturelle, Paris, France. Casts from various parts of the world.

Naturhistorisches Museum, Humboldt University, East Berlin, East Germany. East African dinosaurs, *Brachiosaurus* and *Kentrosaurus*.

Senckenberg Museum, Frankfurt, West Germany. Originals and casts of North American dinosaurs.

Stuttgart Naturhistorisches Museum, Stuttgart, West Germany. *Plateosaurus* and other German dinosaurs in spectacular new mounts.

University Museum, Oxford, England. English Jurassic dinosaurs, including the first *Megalosaurus*.

Academy of Natural Sciences, Philadelphia, Pennsylvania. Various North American Cretaceous dinosaurs.

American Museum of Natural History, New York. Large collection of "classic" North American dinosaurs.

Buffalo Museum of Science, Buffalo, New York. Casts of US dinosaurs.

Carnegie Museum of Natural History, Pittsburgh, Pennsylvania. Upper Jurassic dinosaurs from Utah and Colorado.

Denver Museum of Natural History, Denver, Colorado. Cretaceous dinosaurs.

Dinosaur National Monument, Jensen, Utah. "Working" display in the Late Jurassic.

Earth Sciences Museum, Provo, Utah. The two largest dinosaurs, *Supersaurus* and *Ultrasaurus*.

Field Museum of Natural History, Chicago, Illinois. Action mount of *Albertosaurus* feeding on a duckbill.

Fort Worth Museum of Science, Fort Worth, Texas. Late Jurassic dinosaurs.

Los Angeles County Museum, Los Angeles, California. Casts of a range of US dinosaurs.

Museum of Comparative Zoology, Cambridge, Massachusetts. Triassic dinosaurs from all parts of the world.

Museum of Northern Arizona, Flagstaff, Arizona. *Coelophysis* and *Scutellosaurus*.

Museum of Paleontology, Berkeley, California. The early crested theropod *Dilophosaurus*.

Museum of the Rockies, Bozeman, Montana. Nests, eggs, young and adults of the duckbill *Maiasaura*.

National Museum of Natural History, Washington, DC. Jurassic and Cretaceous dinosaurs from the midwest.

National Museum of Natural Sciences, Ottawa, Ontario. Late Cretaceous dinosaurs from Alberta.

Peabody Museum of Natural History, New Haven, Connecticut. *Deinonychus* and other Cretaceous forms.

Redpath, Museum, Montreal, Quebec. Small Canadian Cretaceous dinosaurs.

Royal Ontario Museum, Toronto, Ontario. Late Cretaceous dinosaurs from Alberta.

Tyrrell Museum of Paleontology, Drumheller, Alberta. Working exhibits; large numbers of local Late Cretaceous dinosaurs.

University of Michigan Exhibit Museum, Ann Arbor, Michigan. Casts of Late Jurassic dinosaurs.

University of Wyoming Geological Museum, Laramie, Wyoming. Jurassic and Cretaceous dinosaurs.

Utah Museum of Natural History, Salt Lake City, Utah. Late Jurassic dinosaurs.

SOUTH AND CENTRAL AMERICA

Museo Argentino de Ciencias Naturales, Buenos Aires, Argentina. Smallest dinosaur *Mussaurus* and one of largest, *Antarctosaurus*.

Museum of La Plata University, La Plata, Argentina. Cast of *Diplodocus*.

Museu Nacional, Rio de Janeiro, Brazil. Several sauropod skeletons.

Natural History Museum, Mexico City, Mexico. Cast of *Diplodocus*.

GLOSSARY

Certain technical names and phrases crop up throughout this book. Below is a guide to what they mean.

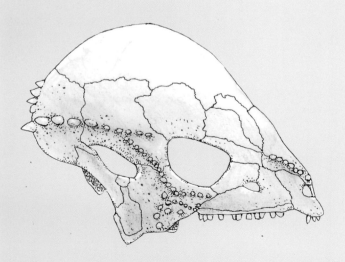

A

Acetabulum: bowl-like socket on the side of the hip girdle for the thigh bone.

Adaptive radiation: the rapid evolutionary expansion of a group, either after a mass extinction, or as a result of the acquisition of a new character.

Aetosaur: a plant-eating thecodontian of the Late Triassic.

Anatomy: the physical make-up of a body, human or animal.

Angiosperm: a flowering plant.

Apatite: a crystalline form of calcium phosphate, a major constituent of bone.

Archosaur: a "ruling reptile"; the group that includes crocodilians, thecodontians, dinosaurs, pterosaurs, and birds.

Assemblage: an associated collection of fossils that may or may not represent a natural fauna.

B

Biology: the study of living things.

Biomechanics: the engineering properties of biological materials and their actions.

C

Cartilage: a flexible hard tissue, like bone, but lacking the crystalline apatite component.

Catastrophism: the view that the history of the Earth and the history of life has been punctuated by crises.

Clade: a natural group in an evolutionary tree, containing all of the descendants of a single common ancestor.

Cladistic analysis: the search for natural groups in classification by means of the search for shared derived characters.

Cladogram: the tree-like image of a classification produced by cladistic analysis.

Classification: a scheme to show the relationships of a group of organisms.

Collagen: a flexible protein that makes up a large part of bone and cartilage.

Community: a group of plants and animals that live together in close association and inter-dependence.

Conservator: a museum technician who repairs and preserves fossils.

Continental drift: the movement of plates of the Earth's crust relative to each other.

Coprolite: fossilised faeces.

Cranium: the part of the skull that covers the brain.

D

Cynodont: an advanced carnivorous mammal-like reptile, on the line to the first true mammals.

Decomposer: an organism that feeds on dead plants and animals and reduces them to soil.

Dentine: the living tissue making up the core of a tooth.

Dermal bone: bone derived late in development from skin-associated tissues; often forming flat sheets of bone.

Dichotomy: a two-way branching point on a cladogram.

Dicynodont: an herbivorous mammal-like reptile with a horny "beak" and reduced teeth.

Digitigrade: walking up on the toes.

E

Ecospace: the broad habitat and range of activities of a species or clade.

Ectothermy: temperature control by external means only, as in fishes, amphibians, and most reptiles.

Embryo: an early developmental stage, within the womb, or within an egg.

Enamel: the hard crystalline outer covering of a tooth.

Endothermy: temperature control by internal means, as in birds and mammals.

Erect posture: stance adopted by dinosaurs, birds and mammals in which the limbs are directly beneath the body.

Extinction: death of a species or other clade.

F

Fauna: the associated animals of a particular area.

Femur: thigh bone.

Fenestra: opening in a skull or other bone.

Fibula: the narrower shin bone running parallel to the tibia.

Fossilization: the processes of preservation of organisms in rocks.

G

Gastrolith: a stomach stone.

Genus: (pl. genera) the larger grouping into which a species is classified; eg, the genus *Homo* for the species *Homo sapiens.*

Geology: the study of the Earth.

Gradualism: the view that the history of the Earth and of life has occurred in a regular progressive way, without major catastrophes.

H

Habitat: the physical and biological "place where an animal lives".

Homeothermy: possession of constant body temperature.

Humerus: the upper arm bone.

K

Keratin: a flexible inert protein that makes hair, feathers, finger nails, claws, beaks, and scales.

L

Ligament: flexible tissues that join bones together.

Lineage: an evolutionary line.

M

Mass extinction: a sudden dying out of many unrelated lineages in all habitats.

Matrix: the background rock that surrounds a fossil.

Monophyletic group: a clade, a natural group that includes all the descendants of a single common ancestor.

N

Node: a branching point in a cladogram.

O

Osteocyte: a bone-making cell.

Outgroup: the group of organisms used to test for derived characters in constructing a cladogram.

P

Palaeontology: the study of ancient life.

Paraphyletic group: a group of organisms that arose from a single common ancestor, but excludes some of the descendants (eg, the Class Reptilia).

Parietal: the skull bones towards the back of the skull roof in the midline.

Petrifacation: 'turning to stone'; the mineral replacement of biological tissues during fossilization.

Phylogeny: an evolutionary tree.

Physiology: the study of how plants and animals work.

Phytosaur: a fish-eating thecodontian of the Late Triassic that looked superficially crocodile-like.

Pleurokinetic joint: the flapping cheek joint seen in advanced ornithopod dinosaurs.

Poikilothermy: the condition of having variable body temperature.

Polyphyletic group: a group of organisms that does not share a common ancestor (eg, the old group Natantia, for fishes and whales).

Preparator: a museum technician who removes fossils from the rock.

Pterosaur: a flying reptile.

R

Radius: a bone of the forearm that runs parallel to the ulna.

Reconstruction: putting flesh on the bones of a fossil.

Restoration: filling in the gaps in a damaged fossil to render it complete.

Rhynchosaur: a beaked herbivorous reptile of the Triassic.

S

Scapula: the shoulder blade.

Scavenger: an animal that feeds on dead animals.

Sedimentary rock: a rock like mudstone, sandstone, or limestone, that formed from sediments laid down on land or underwater.

Skeleton: the bony support of a vertebrate body.

Species: a natural breeding group.

Sprawling posture: the stance of an animal that has its legs projecting to the sides, as in a lizard or a salamander.

Squamosal: the bone in the back angles of the skull roof.

Stromatolite: a biological structure made from alternate layers of mud and blue-green algae.

Synapomorphy: a shared derived character.

T

Taxonomy: the classification and phylogeny of organisms.

Tendon: the tough connective tissue that attaches a muscle to a bone.

Thecodontian: a basal archosaur of the Triassic.

Thermoregulation: temperature control.

Tibia: larger shin bone that runs parallel to the fibula.

Trace fossil: a trackway, burrow, or other impression in rock of the activity of an extinct mammal.

Trochanter: a projection on the femur for the attachment of muscles.

U

Ulna: a bone of the forearm that runs parallel to the radius.

V

Vertebra: a bone of the backbone.

Vertebrate: animal with vertebrae; a fish, amphibian, reptile, bird, or mammal.

INDEX

Page numbers in italics
refer to illustrations

CREDITS

Quarto would like to thank the following for their help in compiling this book. Every effort has been made to obtain copyright clearance, and we do apologize if any omissions have been made.

p6, Ann Ronan Picture Library; p7, Imitor; p9, Ann Ronan Picture Library; pp10-11, Ann Ronan Picture Library; p12, Ann Ronan Picture Library; p13, Joyce Pope; p14, Quarto; p22, British Museum Natural History, London; p25, Field Museum of Natural History, Chicago; p28, R.A. Preston — Mafham Premaphotos; p30, Dr. Michael Benton; p31, Dr. Michael Benton; p36, Oxford University Museum; p37, Quarto; p40, Dr. Michael Benton; p41, Dr. Michael Benton; p42, top left: Steve Hutt Museum of Geology, Isle of Wight; top right: Joyce Pope; bottom right: Kathie Atkinson Oxford Scientific Films; p43, Quarto; p44, Quarto; p45, Bayerische Staatssammlung für Paläontologie und historische Geologie, Munich; p48, top: Ann Ronan Picture Library; bottom: Ann Ronan Picture Library; p49, Dr. Michael Benton; p50, Dr. Michael Benton; p52, top left: Dr. Michael Benton; top & bottom right: Institut Royal des Sciences Naturelles de Belgique; p53, Dr. Michael Benton; pp54, 55 & 56, Dr. Michael Benton; p57, top left: Dr. Michael Benton; top right: GSF; pp60 & 61, Dr.Michael Benton; p62, GSF; p63, Dr. Michael Benton; p64, top left: GSF; bottom right: Dr. Michael Benton; p65, left & top right: Dr. Michael Benton; bottom right: Oxford University Museum; pp66 & 67, Dr. Michael Benton; p70, Quarto; p71, Dr. Michael Benton; p72, Dr. Michael Benton; p73, Quarto; p74, Ann Ronan Picture Library; p77, bottom: Ann Ronan Picture Library; p81, Quarto; p82, British Museum Natural History, London; p83, Tyrell Museum of Palaeontology; p85, British Museum Natural History, London; p86, Quarto; p90, Joyce Pope; p91, Quarto; p92, left: Ann Ronan Picture Library; top right: Joyce Pope; p96, Tyrell Museum of Palaeontology; p98, Tyrell Museum of Palaeontology; p100, British Museum Natural History, London; p103, top: Smithsonian Institution; bottom: Tyrell Museum of Palaeontology; p109, British Museum Natural History, London; pp112 & 113, Ann Ronan Picture Library; p119, Moscow Academy of Sciences; p120, left: Ann Ronan Picture Library; pp120-121, Denver Museum of Natural History Photo Archives; p123, Tyrell Museum of Palaeontology; p124, E. Coppola Oxford Scientific Films; p126, Joyce Pope; p127, Kathie Atkinson Oxford Scientific Films; p128, NPHA; p129, Dr. Michael Benton; p131, Science Photo Library; p136, British Museum Natural History, London.

Dinosaur Reconstructions: Graham Rosewarne; Skeletal diagrams: Jim Robins; charts and diagrams: Janos Marrfy, Sally Launder, Kevin Maddison, David Kemp.